BASIC
MADE
EASY

BASIC
MADE
EASY

A Guide to Programming Microcomputers and Minicomputers

Don Cassel
Richard Swanson

Humber College of
Applied Arts and Technology

RESTON PUBLISHING COMPANY, INC., Reston, Virginia
A Prentice-Hall Company

Library of Congress Cataloging in Publication Data

Cassel, Don
    Basic made easy.

    Includes index.
    1. Basic (computer program language).
    2. Micro-computers—programming.
    3. Minicomputers—programming.
I. Swanson, Richard—joint author. II. Title.
QA76.73.B3C36   001.64'24   80-12626
ISBN 0-8359-0399-0
ISBN 0-8359-0398-2 (pbk.)

©1980 by
RESTON PUBLISHING COMPANY, INC., Reston, Virginia 22090
A Prentice-Hall Company

10   9   8   7   6   5   4   3   2

Printed in the United States of America.

Preface

The recent popularity of micro and minicomputers has led to a significent increase in the use of the BASIC language. This book addresses this popularity by offering an introduction to BASIC at the level of the first time user.

BASIC Made Easy assumes no background in either computers or programming. We begin by introducing the reader to the various components of a computer system. This chapter provides a terminology base which is so important to any user of a computer system whether small or large. Common input/output devices, like display screens, keyboards, card readers, printers, disk and tape, are explained without getting too technical. Following hardware is a brief discussion of software dealing with commonly used programs such as operating systems, interpreters, utilities and application programs.

One of the most difficult aspects of learning to program is problem solving. In our experience students of programming have far more difficulty learning how to approach the problem than they do in learning the statements of the BASIC language. For this reason an entire chapter is devoted to problem solving. Although we would have liked to use an approach which leads to structured programs we feel that flowcharting is a more natural approach to problem solving for most BASIC implementations. Therefore, Chapter 2 discusses flowcharting methods and shows how to solve a variety of problems using flowcharts as the problem solving tool.

The remainder of the book deals with the BASIC language. Each component of the language is introduced carefully with plenty of examples to help the reader see how a new feature of the language is used. These examples are both individual statements and complete programs which show input data and output results. We would encourage students to run some of these programs on their computer and observe the results firsthand.

A new programmer will invariably make plenty of errors on the first attempt at programming. To assist in finding these mistakes we have included, in each chapter, a section of *Common Errors* made by the learning programmer (and also by more experienced ones).

In addition to the chapters on BASIC is Chapter 7 which discusses *Debugging and Testing.* This comes at the point when programs are becoming sufficiently complex that a student may not find correcting errors to be self-evident. This chapter explains how to desk check and trace errors in program logic.

Most chapters end with a series of problems. In the classroom environment these may be used for assignments. For the reader who is studying BASIC independently the problems may be used as self testing material to check your understanding of each chapter.

Finally, the elements of BASIC which we have chosen are common to most BASIC interpreters. If there is any exception to this it will be primarily in the *Files* chapter as an introduction to the Basic language. *BASIC Made Easy* is suitable for use on virtually any computer.

Contents

BASIC
MADE
EASY

1
Introduction
to
Minicomputers
and
Microcomputers

1

This book is about computer programming. Computers do not understand languages such as English. Instead, they have their own languages. One of these languages is BASIC, which is used to communicate with the computer and to instruct it how to solve problems for us. In order to understand some of the capabilities that the computer has, we need an understanding of the hardware and software that we are going to use. Hardware refers to the physical components of the computer, and software refers to the programs that are provided with the computer to assist us in using the hardware. In this book, we will limit our discussion of hardware and software to minicomputers and microcomputers.

Until very recently, computers were feasible for only large business organizations, universities and government. This was due to the high cost of computers and the need for a large staff of support personnel to use them effectively. Today, this has all changed. The cost of computers has decreased to the extent that virtually every business can afford one. Computers are even available for home use for the price of a modest stereo system. Using the computer has become simpler. Many small computers can be used by people with a minimum of technical training.

Minicomputers and microcomputers are at the forefront of developments leading to the inexpensive computer. A minimum configuration microcomputer costs less than $1000 and a minicomputer less than $15,000. These are general cost figures and vary greatly from one specific system to another.

HARDWARE–COMPONENTS OF A COMPUTER SYSTEM

A computer consists of a number of individual components. The processor does the work of arithmetic calculations and decision making. Attached to the processor are various input and output devices. The input devices supply data to the processor for processing. Output devices store the results of the processing or communicate the results to the person using the computer. Every computer needs at least one input device and one output device. Figure 1.1 shows a computer system with a variety of input/output devices. This system has each device in a separate frame, which is connected by cables to the central processor. Figure 1.2 shows a "personal use" microcomputer where the processor and input/output devices are all mounted in the same frame; in this computer, additional devices may be externally attached to the processor.

FIGURE 1.1 Minicomputer System *(Courtesy of Cincinnati Milacron)*

FIGURE 1.2 Microcomputer System *(Courtesy of Commodore Business Machine)*

PROCESSORS

The processor (Figure 1.3) is the heart or, as some would put it, the brain of a computer system. This is where all the action is. The processor follows the instructions of the program to solve a specific problem. The processor accesses data from input devices, acts on the data by making comparisons and doing arithmetic, and then places the results on an output device. The processor does not do this on its own initiative but follows the instructions given it in the program written by a human programmer.

A processor is described in terms of its size and speed. Size refers to the number of bytes or characters (sometimes words) that the processor can store. This affects the size of program that can be stored in the processor for execution. In microcomputers, the storage is called RAM, meaning Random Access Memory. Sizes may range from 4K, meaning 4000 (K = 1000) or more precisely 4096, bytes to as high as 2M (M = 1,000,000) bytes. Typical intermediate sizes are 16K, 32K, 64K, 128K and 256K, depending on the design of the processor. Most processors can be expanded beyond their minimum storage size. For a price of course.

Some processors also have ROM, Read Only Memory. This memory contains a program or programs that have been recorded by the computer manufacturer. ROM may include programs such as the BASIC language interpreter and the computer's control program,

FIGURE 1.3   HP 1000 F-Series Computer
A processor with 64K bytes of memory expandable to 512K internally and 1280K externally. *(Courtesy Hewlett-Packard Data Systems)*

which controls the activity of all other programs as well as input/output operations.

Speed refers to the time that it takes the processor to do a given operation. One measurement is cycle time, for which 250 nanoseconds is typical; a nanosecond is one-billionth of a second. A more meaningful measurement is the minimum instruction execution time, which is the time required to execute a very simple instruction, such as an add; one microsecond or one-millionth of a second is typical here.

INPUT/OUTPUT DEVICES

A large variety of input and output devices exist for use with the processor. Figure 1.4 shows a symbolic diagram representing a number of such devices. Most computers use only a few of these, many only two or three.

PUNCHED-CARD READER

At one time, the punched card was the primary means of supplying input to a computer. Today with the mini-computer and microcomputer, it is fast disappearing. However, since it is still in use, we are covering it here.

Figure 1.5 shows the 80 column punched card, sometimes called the IBM card. It was invented by Herman Hollerith in 1880. Alphabetic, numeric and some special characters can be punched on

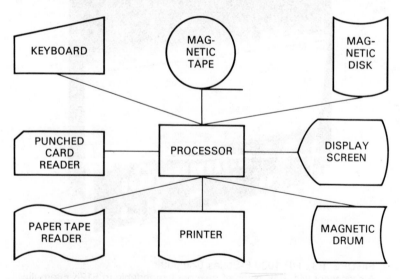

FIGURE 1.4   A Symbolic Diagram of Various Input/Output Devices

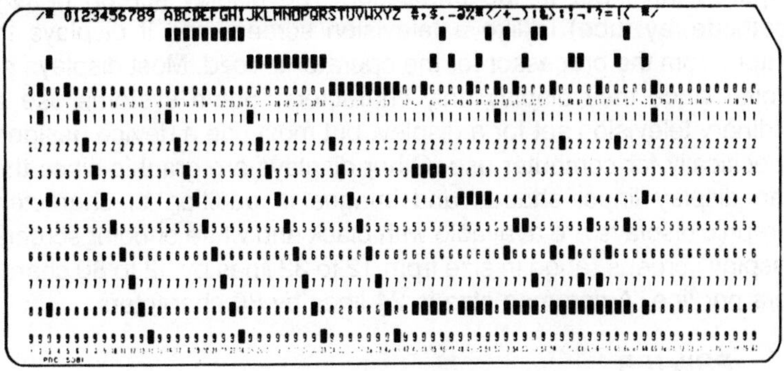

FIGURE 1.5   Hollerith Punched Card

the card by means of a keypunch machine. Once the cards are punched, they are fed into the computer by a card reader. The card reader reads the Hollerith code and sends it to the processor, where it is processed by the program.

DISPLAY SCREEN AND KEYBOARD

The display screen and keyboard is becoming the most popular input/output device since it combines both input and output in the same frame. Shown in Figure 1.6, the device consists of two basic

FIGURE 1.6   Display Screen and Keyboard *(Courtesy of Cincinnati Milacron)*

components. The keyboard, which is used in typewriter-like fashion, supplies the input to the processor. The display screen or CRT (cathode-ray tube) is like a television screen, and it displays the output from the processor for the operator to read. Most displays are digital since they display only characters. Some systems use an ordinary television set for a display, but most use a device designed specifically for computer use. Other displays are graphic since they can display lines, shapes and images in addition to characters. Graphic displays are available with black and white or color screens. Display screens range in size from 12 to 32 lines by 32 to 80 characters per line. A common size is 24 lines by 80 characters.

PRINTER

One problem with the display is that it does not produce a permanent record of the computer output. This is overcome by having a printer attached for output. A printer like the one in Figure 1.7 prints 132 characters per line at a speed of 30 characters per second. The print mechanism uses a dot matrix to form the character. Although this printer has a keyboard for input to the computer, most printers do not. Typewriters, wire matrix, daisy wheel and thermal and chain printers are all used by various computers. These range in speed from 10 characters per second to 1000 lines per minute.

FIGURE 1.7   DEC Writer II Keyboard Printer *(Courtesy Heath Company)*

MAGNETIC TAPE

A magnetic tape drive is a device that either reads or writes onto the surface of a mylar tape. The mylar tape has a coating of ferrous oxide on one side, as shown in Figure 1.8, which permits it to be magnetized. The magnetic tape drive records information in magnetic spots along this tape.

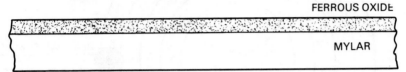

FERROUS OXIDE

MYLAR

FIGURE 1.8   Magnetic Tape

Figure 1.9 shows how these magnetic spots are used to represent data along the surface of the tape. A typical tape consists of nine tracks of bits. A single row across these nine tracks represents one character of data. A typical tape drive can pack 1600 characters of information onto 1 inch of tape. This capacity is known as density and is referred to in terms of characters per inch. A magnetic tape reader can read this data up to speeds of 180,000 characters per second. Magnetic tape is a medium-speed device capable of storing large amounts of information.

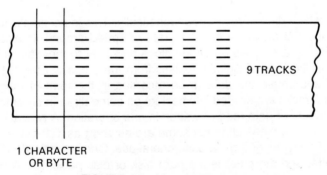

9 TRACKS

1 CHARACTER
OR BYTE

FIGURE 1.9   Magnetic Tape

Some microcomputers, particularly the ones for personal use, employ audio cassette tapes and drives for magnetic tape storage. These are inexpensive and provide a medium-speed method of storing and retrieving data.

MAGNETIC DISK

A disk consists of a circular platter covered with a magnetic coating. The surface is divided into concentric tracks (Figure 1.10)

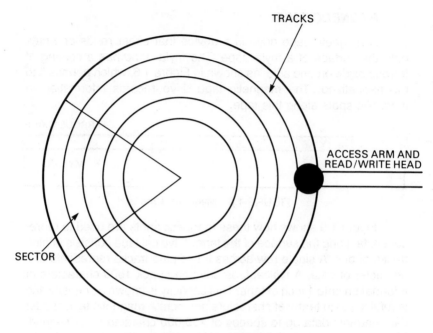

FIGURE 1.10 Magnetic Disk

upon which data is recorded magnetically. This is accomplished by spinning the disk at a constant rate of speed around its axis and positioning a read/write head in close proximity to the disk surface. Data in the form of digital impulses from the processor travel to the head and cause the data to be recorded in the form of magnetic spots. Tracks are divided into sectors on some disks in order to limit the amount of data read or written in one operation. A typical sector length is 256 bytes although some are as short as 128 bytes.

Two types of disks are in general use. One is the floppy disk or diskette, and the other is the hard disk or disk pack. The floppy is used primarily by microcomputer users, as shown in Figure 1.11. These diskettes are compact, easy to install, and have a medium data capacity. Floppys can be either the 5 inch minidisk or the standard 8 inch disk. The minidisk has a capacity of about 85K whereas a regular floppy generally stores 250K for single density and 500K for dual density. Some hard disks may also be used on the microcomputer.

Hard disks are more frequently used on the minicomputer although some minicomputers also use floppys. Usually, a hard disk consists of several metal platters, coated with a magnetic substance and mounted together in a plastic container, called a disk pack,

FIGURE 1.11   A Floppy-Disk Drive *(Courtesy Cromemco Incorporated)*

FIGURE 1.12   PDP-11 Dual-Drive Disk Pack Subsystem *(Courtesy of Digital Equipment Corporation)*

which protects the disk from damage. Figure 1.12 shows a dual-drive disk pack in a minicomputer system. Disk packs come in a great variety of capacities, ranging from 5M bytes to over 100M bytes on some large systems.

Disks are used in most computer systems because of their direct access capabilities. Devices such as magnetic tapes offer comparable storage capacity and speed but are sequential in nature. This means that, to access any record on tape, all of the previous records must first be read. For many computer applications, this simply takes too much time. Disks provide the solution to this since they can directly access any record without reading other data on the disk. Direct access capability is of particular value to interactive and on-line systems where response time is a critical factor in system performance.

PAPER TAPE

Figure 1.13 shows a length of paper tape used for input and output on some systems. The tape is 1 in. wide and comes in rolls of up to several hundred feet in length. The tape is punched like a card although the codes used are different. Records can be of any length whereas cards are limited to 80 characters. Its main attractions are low cost and compact storage. Data are stored sequentially, like magnetic tape, but paper tape cannot be reused. Paper tape readers can read 50 characters per second whereas the punch is much slower at 10 characters per second.

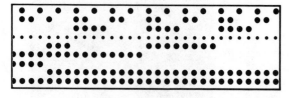

FIGURE 1.13   Paper Tape

COMPUTER SOFTWARE

Most computers are supplied with software programs to assist in the use of the hardware. The software can be supplied in two basically different ways. The first method, used primarily in microcomputers, is the use of Read Only Memory (ROM), where the software is built into the hardware on a memory chip. The second method, which is the most common, supplies the software programs on a magnetic tape or disk; these programs are loaded into the computer when they are needed.

Regardless of how the software is supplied, there are several categories of software programs. These are the supervisor, interpreters, utilities and application packages.

SUPERVISOR

This program is supplied with most computers and is variously called the monitor, nucleus or control program. The supervisor directs all activities going on in the processor: it loads programs into memory, gives them control for execution, and assists in input/output operations. In timesharing systems, the supervisor controls the activities of several simultaneous users of the computer, giving each a sufficient amount of computer time to do his job.

INTERPRETERS

These are programs that interpret a high-level language into machine language. Each computer has one machine language, which is usually quite technical in nature. To simplify the process of communicating with the computer, several high-level languages are available that are easier to understand and use than the machine language. The high-level language we are using is BASIC. Other high-level languages are COBOL, Fortran, ALGOL, PL/I, APL and RPG II. Not all computers understand these languages. Some only use one or two whereas others use them all. Each language used requires a separate interpreter or compiler; this adds to the cost of the software and it occupies more storage space in the computer hardware.

UTILITIES

Utilities are software programs that do repetitive input/output operations. This relieves the programmer of the responsibility of writing these programs each time they are needed. Some common utility programs are tape to disk, disk to tape, tape to printer, disk to printer and sort/merge. For example, instead of writing a program to print the contents of a disk file, the programmer simply codes a few control statements that are used by the utility to read the correct file and to produce the required output.

APPLICATION PACKAGES

Today's computer users, particularly the smaller businesses, have a lot of common processing requirements. These include areas such as accounts receivable, accounts payable, inventory control and sales analysis. Instead of each user writing his own program, the computer manufacturer makes prewritten programs available for these applications. Since the methods used for accounting are essentially the same for everyone, a single application package for accounting can be used by each company. Minor, individual differences can usually be incorporated by making changes in the package; large changes require the writing of new programs. These application packages are available at extra cost from most computer companies. In addition to the manufacturer, specialized software houses market this type of program for the computer user.

2
Using Flowcharts to Solve Programming Problems

Programming problems vary in degree of difficulty; some are quite simple whereas others are very complex, requiring considerable planning to complete a logical, clear and efficient program. One of the methods of organizing the logic of a program is called flowcharting.

A flowchart is made up of a series of symbols, each with a descriptive comment, joined by flow lines. The steps that are necessary to solve a programming problem are written in the appropriate sequence to achieve the desired results. Figure 2.1 shows the various symbols and components that may be used in the creation of a flowchart.

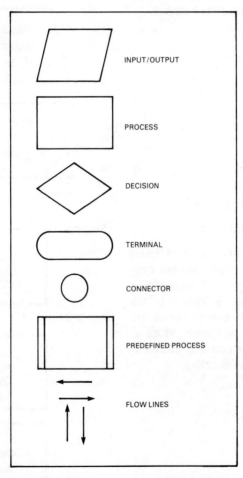

FIGURE 2-1   Flowchart Symbols

FLOWCHART SYMBOLS

INPUT/OUTPUT

Description   *Symbol*

This symbol is used to represent the action of bringing data into the program or sending information to an output device. The data can be supplied to the program via a keyboard or from a file, which has been stored on an available input/output device.

Examples

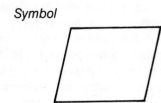

Read
Account
Data

Input
from
Keyboard

PROCESS

Description   *Symbol*

A process is an imperative action (a command) that does not indicate any transfer of data into or from the machine. Typical of this kind of activity are: calculate the sum of two numbers, store a value for later use and calculate an average by dividing.

Examples

Add 1 to
Counter

Calculate
Average

DECISION

Description

The decision block indicates that a comparison is to be made. Based on the result of the comparison, control passes to one of two places in the logic.

Symbol

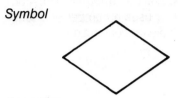

Examples

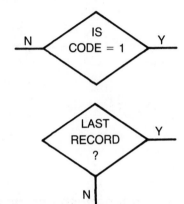

TERMINAL

Description

In order to indicate the beginning and the end of a flowchart, the terminal block is used. It does not represent an active command but is useful in defining the start and finish points in a large flowchart.

Symbol

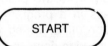

Example

START

CONNECTOR

Description

The long flow lines, which may be employed to join distant blocks in a flowchart, may be avoided by the use of this symbol. It indicates the transfer of

Symbol

control from one section of the flowchart to another. The connector uses a number or a letter to indicate connection.

Example

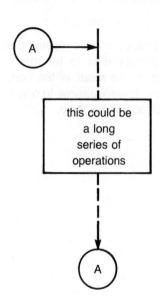

PREDEFINED PROCESS

Description

This symbol represents a procedure that is presumably too large or complex to be included as a part of the current logic. One method commonly used to incorporate the predefined process in a program is called a subroutine, which will be discussed in detail in Chapter 9.

Symbol

Example

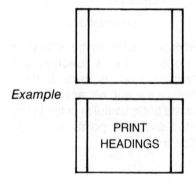

FLOW LINES

Description

The symbols in a flowchart are joined by flow lines. The normal progression is downward or to the right. If the direction is to the

Symbol

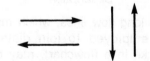

left or toward the top of the flowchart, then arrows must be used.
Arrows may be used on any line
if it results in a clearer flowchart.
Figure 2.2 illustrates some
common flowcharting conventions.

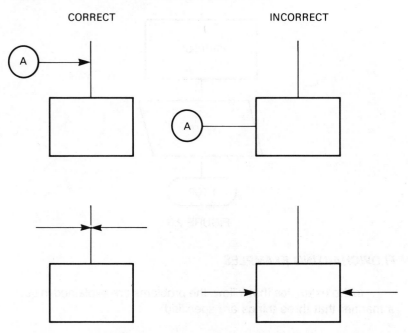

FIGURE 2.2   Flowcharting Conventions

SAMPLE FLOWCHARTS

Figure 2.3 illustrates a simple flowchart. This "typical" flowchart
illustrates the reading of one set of input data, the processing of that
data, and the written output of the result. Notice that the blocks are
"executed" from the beginning to the end in the order indicated by
the flow lines and that each block is performed only once since no
indication is given that the steps are repeated.

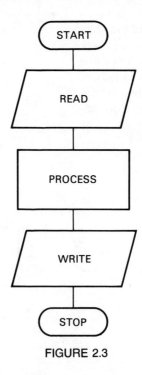

FIGURE 2.3

FLOWCHARTING EXAMPLES

In the examples that follow, the problems are explained in such a manner that three things are specified:

1. The input that is available for the program to read,

2. Any specific operations to be performed on the data, and

3. The output that is required as a result of the processing.

Example 1: Product of Two Numbers

Two numbers are to be read into a program. The product of the numbers is to be calculated, and the numbers and their product printed.

The flowchart in Figure 2.4 represents a solution to this problem.

NOTES ON FIGURE 2.4. The flowchart in Figure 2.4 indicates the following sequence:

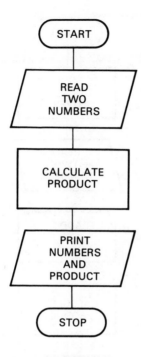

FIGURE 2.4

1.   The two numbers are read from an input device and are made available to the program.

2.   Their product is calculated.

3.   The numbers and their product are printed as output.

4.   The program is terminated.

Example 2:   Repeating Flowchart Steps

Ten pairs of numbers are to be read into a program. For each set, the product is to be calculated and printed along with the original numbers.

The flowchart for this problem must allow for ten repetitions of the steps (Figure 2.5).

NOTES ON FIGURE 2.5.   When first dealing with the concept of computer programming, we are often guilty of assuming that the computer "knows" what we want to do. However, since the computer is simply a machine, it cannot know what we want any more than a car knows its destination.

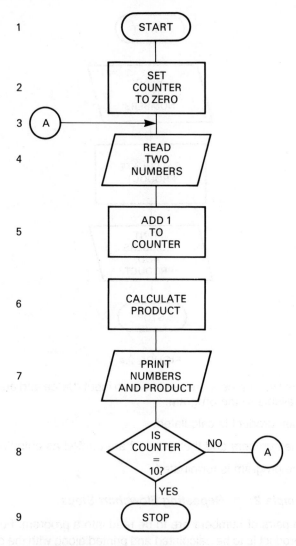

FIGURE 2.5   Reading Ten Pairs of Numbers

Most of us have used an adding machine or a calculator. The first step in calculating the total of a set of numbers is to clear the machine of any previous values. In the same way, we must set the starting value of any accumulator or counter, which is important to the logic of the program. This initialization is done in the block 2. After a set of data is read, the counter is incremented by one, as indicated by block 5. Its original value was zero; its value is now 1. Blocks 6 and 7 are responsible for calculating and printing the desired results, and block 8 asks a question:

IS THE VALUE OF THE COUNTER = 10?

Since the value of the counter is only at 1, the answer to the question is "NO." When the answer is NO, control is directed to the connector block A, which is found entering the logic at block 3. After a set of data is read, the counter is again incremented by one and this time becomes 2. The same negative response answers the question at block 8. Control is again sent to the connector symbol A, and the steps are repeated. This repetition continues until the value of the counter does equal 10, indicating that ten pairs of numbers have been read, processed and written. At this time, the logic indicates that the program is to be terminated.

Example 3:   Sum of 1 to 100

Find the sum of all the integers from 1 to 100. The required output will be the sum of 100 numbers:

$$1 + 2 + 3 + ... + 97 + 98 + 99 + 100 = ?$$

The flowchart is shown in Figure 2.6.

NOTES ON FIGURE 2.6.   The method used in the flowchart is to start a number (NUM) at 1 and add it to a counter (SUM). Increase the number by 1 and add the new value to the counter. This would be followed by the values 3, 4, 5, etc. up to the value of 100. When the value 100 has been added, the problem has been solved, and the answer can be printed. No reading at all is done in the program, and only one writing is done, at the end of the logic just before the entire operation is terminated.

Once the logic has been designed, changes could easily be made to accomodate finding the sum of integers up to a different number, such as 500 or 1000. The only alteration would be to change the question at the end to look for the appropriate value.

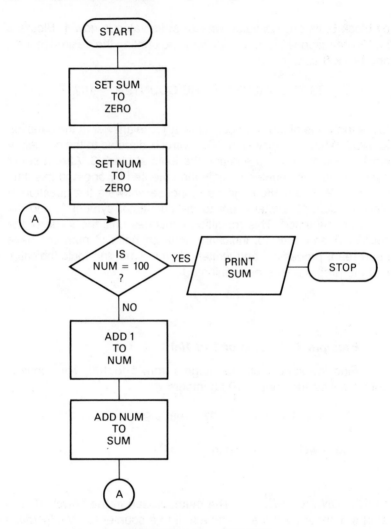

FIGURE 2.6 Sum of 1 to 100

lated. At the end of the file, the average is calculated and printed. In this problem, many values are brought into the program, but very little output is required.

Example 5: Printing an Invoice

A customer purchased several items at a warehouse. For each item sold, the item number, the quantity sold and the cost of each item are available. An invoice is required, showing the item number,

Example 4: Calculating Averages

Read in a set of ten numbers and determine the average of those numbers. The only output required is the average.

The flowchart is shown in Figure 2.7.

NOTES ON FIGURE 2.7. The total of all the incoming numbers must be known before the average can be calculated. This total is available only after all the numbers have been read and accumu-

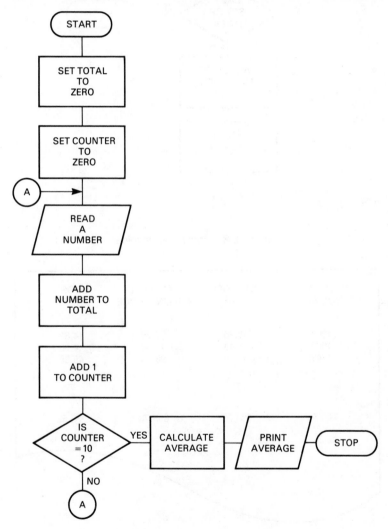

FIGURE 2.7 Finding an Average

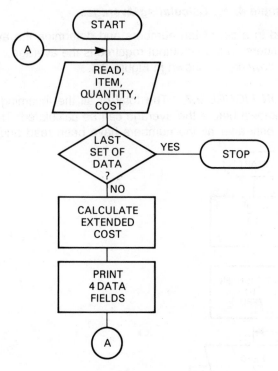

FIGURE 2.8   Printing an Invoice

ITEM NUMBER	EXTENDED COST	EXTENDED SELLING PRICE	GROSS PROFIT
1204	42.96	57.78	14.82
1689	12.48	16.48	4.00
1743	51.00	96.95	45.95
—	—	—	—
—	—	—	—
—	—	—	—
—	—	—	—
TOTAL	594.26	859.78	265.52

FIGURE 2.9   Total Accumulation

the quantity, the unit cost and the extended cost (the quantity multiplied by the unit cost;.

The flowchart in Figure 2.8 represents a solution to the problem.

NOTES ON FIGURE 2.8.   This logic shows how a problem could be handled when the number of incoming records is unknown. It is quite common in programming that a program may be used repeatedly with a different number of input records each time. In such a case, it is accepted practice to place a record at the end of the incoming data, which is a signal that no more data is to be processed. Examples of possible programming methods are shown in Chapter 7; however, in determining the logic necessary to solve the problem, we must simply recognize that such action is possible.

The decision block is responsible for determining whether a record is an item sold or the end-of-file indicator. If a record is not the last, a calculation is necessary to determine the extended cost. At this point, all the information is available to print the required output, i.e., item number, quantity, unit cost and extended cost. Control is passed back to the connector block, and the actions are repeated until a "YES" answer is obtained to the question:

IS THIS THE LAST SET OF DATA?

Example 6:   *Accumulating Totals*

The ABC Wholesale Company keeps a record of all products sold by recording the item number, quantity sold, unit cost and selling price. Prepare a report showing the output in Figure 2.9.

Notice the titles shown at the top and the totals at the bottom after all other lines have been printed. Extended cost is the product of quantity and unit cost. Extended selling price is the product of quantity and selling price. Gross profit is the difference between extended cost and extended selling price.

The logic could be shown in a flowchart, as in Figure 2.10.

NOTES ON FIGURE 2.10.   Several of the requirements in this problem differ from previous examples: headings, or titles, are to be printed before any of the data is printed; total values are required after all data has been processed. The action symbol representing the printing of the headings is shown at the top of the flowchart, where it is done once, and control is never sent back to that point again.

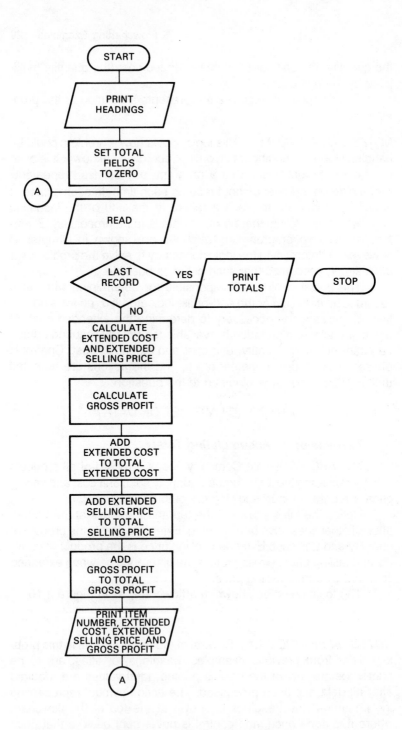

FIGURE 2.10 Total Accumulation

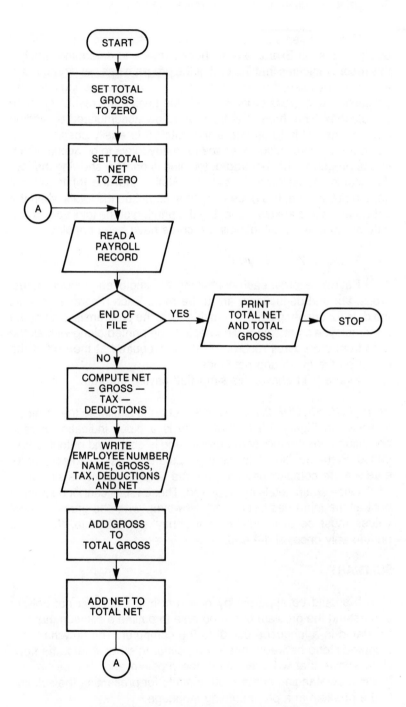

FIGURE 2.11   A Simple Payroll Problem

The four items of data are read into the logic via the READ block, and, as in Example 3, a check is made to determine whether this record indicates that the end of the program has been reached. If this is not the case, the extended cost and extended selling price are calculated, and gross profit is determined using the results of these calculations. The three total fields are now accumulated by adding each of the fields to its respective total. It is easily possible for a computer to have sufficient space for many totals to be accumulated in one program. The required output line is printed, showing the four data items requested in Figure 2.7. Notice that the totals are not printed at this time. It is necessary to accumulate the totals when the individual values are available, but the printing of the total values can only be done when all incoming records have been handled.

Example 7:   Payroll

Payroll records, each containing an employee number, name, gross, tax and deductions, are to be read. Each record represents the data for one employee. From this data, the program is to compute the employee's net salary. The net is to be printed along with all the data from the payroll record. Totals are required at the end of the report on the gross and net fields.

Figure 2.11 shows this simplified payroll program.

NOTES ON FIGURE 2.11.   This flowchart is similar to the "typical" flowchart in Figure 2.3 in that there is a block indicating a read operation near the top, some processing is done, and output is produced. Some additional flowchart steps are necessary to accommodate a more complex problem, but the general activity is similar.

Once again, totals are required. These totals cannot be printed until all the input has been read. However, whereas gross and net values must be accumulated while they are available, totals are printed only once, at the end.

SUMMARY

It should be apparent by now that it is important not only to understand the problem but to be able to outline a solution that can be stated in a language useful to the computer. The flowchart is a stepping stone between these two points. In other words, the flowchart shows that we understand the problem and that we have a basic understanding of the requirements for presenting the solution to the problem in a programming language.

The examples are intended to show the construction of a flow-chart and the terminology used to specify the various steps in the logic. It should be understood, however, that no one flowchart is capable of representing the solution to all programming problems: each problem is unique. A change in the input or the requirements can result in a complete change in the solution. It is important that the programmer be flexible and recognize those elements of a flowchart that are similar from one problem to another without overlooking those aspects of the problem that are unique.

The more problems we are successful in solving, the less difficult it is for us to solve future problems. A good programmer is not necessarily one who has attended many lectures or read many books on the subject but is one who has applied himself to solving many problems and writing programs for them. It is in this way that our abilities are developed. In short, practice, practice, practice!

QUESTIONS

1.   Indicate which symbol would specify the following actions by writing the proper letter in the space provided.

_E_ Connector
_A_ Multiply
_B_ Input/Output
_A_ Process
_D_ Stop
_C_ Decision
_D_ Terminal
_A_ Add
_B_ Read
_A_ Subtract
_A_ Divide
_D_ Start
_B_ Print
_A_ Calculate
_C_ Comparison
_D_ End of File

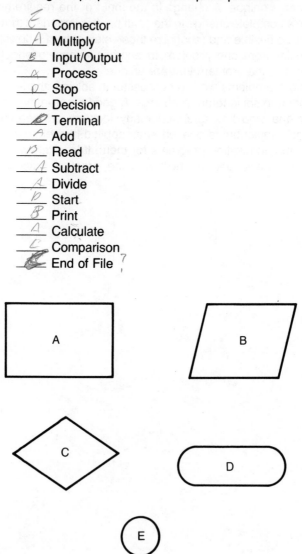

2. Assume that the flow of the logic is at block 1 in each of the following diagrams. Indicate which block would be the next one done.

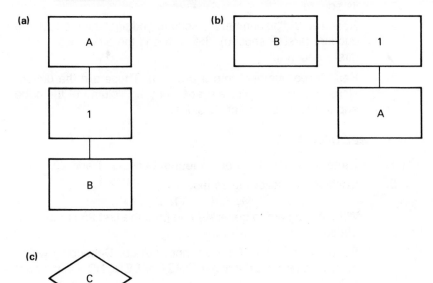

(a)

```
┌─────────┐
│    A    │
└────┬────┘
┌────┴────┐
│    1    │
└────┬────┘
┌────┴────┐
│    B    │
└─────────┘
```

(b)

```
┌─────────┐    ┌─────────┐
│    B    ├────┤    1    │
└─────────┘    └────┬────┘
               ┌────┴────┐
               │    A    │
               └─────────┘
```

(c)

```
   ╱╲
  ╱ C ╲
  ╲   ╱
   ╲╱
┌────┴────┐   ┌─────────┐   ┌─────────┐
│    1    ├───┤    A    ├───┤    B    │
└─────────┘   └─────────┘   └─────────┘
```

3. If you were to include punctuation in the following flowchart block, would END OF FILE be followed by a question mark or a period?

```
   ╱─────────╲
  ╱   END     ╲
  ╲    OF     ╱
   ╲  FILE   ╱
    ╲───────╱
```

   The following problems are divided into sections of increasing difficulty. Section A is the easiest, section D is the most difficult. In each case, construct a flowchart to illustrate a solution to the problem.

SECTION A

1. Read a 3-digit number (100 – 999); print the number and its square.

2. Read two 3-digit numbers; calculate and print the product, the quotient (first ÷ second), the sum and the difference (first - second).

3. Read three numbers into a program. These are the dimensions of a cube. Calculate and print the volume of the cube and the total area of all its sides.

SECTION B

1. Generate a list of the odd integers between 1 and 20.

2. Consider the following series:
$$1, 2, 4, 7, 11, 16, \ldots$$
Write a program to generate and print the first 25 numbers in the series.

3. Read two numbers from an input device. Depending which number is larger, print either FIRST or SECOND. Do not print both words.

SECTION C

1. Each data record contains a student number and the number of days that the student has been absent. Print the student number and the days absent for any student absent 9 or more days.

2. Manhatten Island was purchased from the Indians in 1626 for $24.00. If the Indians had invested the money at 6% interest compounded annually, what would be the value of the investment at the end of the following years: 1690, 1790, 1890 and 1990?

3. A salesman has made many sales. He wants to know how many were $100.00 or less, how many between $100.00 and $200.00 and how many were over $200.00. Each data record contains an invoice number and the sale amount.

SECTION D

1.   An apartment house has 200 units. With a monthly rental of $220 per unit, all apartments are rented. For each $2.50 increase in monthly rent, one unit will become vacant; for example, if the rent is $222.50, 199 units will be rented. The owner wishes to maximize his income and will therefore increase the rent to the point where total rent is at a maximum. Construct a flowchart to determine that rent, the number of units that will be rented and the total monthly revenue.

2.   A class of students is represented by data records, each containing student number, age and average grade. Print the data for all students 19 or older who have an average of 95% or higher. At the end of the list, show the total number of students, the number of students printed and thé percentage of students printed.

3.   Print a class list from data records containing student number, number of subjects and average grade. At the end, print the number of students and the class average.

3
Basic
Programming
Fundamentals

Every statement in the BASIC language consists of some primary elements that apply to each statement. These elements are:

nnnnn   KEYWORD   PARAMETERS

A BASIC statement consists of (1) a statement number represented by nnnnn, (2) a keyword that specifies the operation to be performed, and (3) parameters that are usually variables, constants or expressions. These parameters further direct the operation to be executed.

An example of a BASIC statement is

10   LET   N = 1

In this statement, 10 is the line number, the word LET is the keyword, and N = 1 constitutes the parameters.

STATEMENT NUMBERS

Every BASIC statement begins with a statement number, which identifies the sequential location of that statement within the program. Each line number must be unique; there cannot be any duplicate line numbers within a program. A line number may be up to five digits in length; however, it is usually more convenient to use fewer digits, particularly for smaller programs. Line numbers must be in ascending order, starting with a low number and working up to a higher number.

When writing a BASIC program, one should allow for additional numbers between each statement number assigned. This can be conveniently accomplished by starting with, for example, statement 10 and then going up in increments of ten. Thus, there is room for nine additional statements between each existing line number. If modifications to the program are necessary, it is quite easy to assign a new line number, for example, line number 15, which will be inserted between statements 10 and 20. Even though statement 15 may be keyed in at the end of the program, following statement 120, the computer will sequence 15 into its proper location between statements 10 and 20.

SPACING

Spaces are not required within BASIC programming statements. Thus, the statement

20IFN=100THEN40

is a valid statement and can be recognized by the computer. In this particular statement, 20 is the statement number; IF is a keyword; N = 100 is a parameter; THEN is a keyword; and 40 is a parameter, indicating the statement number to be executed if this comparison is true.

Even though this statement is valid, it is preferable to write BASIC statements with spaces in order to make them more readable. A better way to write this statement is:

20 IF N=100 THEN 40

Spacing not only increases readability but also makes debugging easier if the program contains errors which must be found and corrected.

COMMENTS

Comments may be included in the BASIC language through the use of the REMARK statement. The format for this statement is:

nnnnn REM comments

An alternate format that may be used is:

nnnnn REMARK comments

An example of a REMARK statement is:

100 REMARK COMPUTE TOTALS BY ITERATION

This statement will appear in the appropriate position within the program, but it will not in itself be an executable statement. That is, statement 100 performs no function in the program other than to print this remark as part of the program listing.

If a comment requires more than one line, a subsequent REMARK statement must be used. An example of this is:

```
50 REM THIS ROUTINE IS ONLY EXECUTED
60 REM THE FIRST TIME INTO THE PROGRAM.
70 REM SUBSEQUENT LOOPS CONTINUE AT
80 REM STATEMENT NUMBER 230.
```

Here, the entire comment requires four lines. Each line must have a statement number followed by the keyword REM. Each statement number must be unique, as with any other statement in BASIC.

Liberal use of REMARK statements is particularly useful in a lengthy program where it is possible that complex routines may not be completely understood by the programmer unless some comments are included to explain how the logic works. REMARKS can also be used to identify various routines by supplying a name to identify each of them. The explanation, of course, is only useful for the reader of the program and in no way influences the computer's operation on the program.

It is possible to branch to the statement number of a REMARK statement. If this is done, the computer will continue looking at subsequent statement numbers until it finds a statement that can be executed. It is not advisable to cause a GO TO to branch to a REMARK statement; rather, it should branch to a statement that is intended to be executed.

VARIABLE NAMES

Almost without exception, every program written in BASIC language requires the use of variable names. These variable names usually represent some numeric value which the program can change as required.

The following examples illustrate the use of variable names in a program. If we are presented with the following, the value of Z could be easily determined.

$$10 \quad \text{LET } Z = 3 + 8$$

Z, of course, is 11. However, if the statement were written as:

$$10 \quad \text{LET } Z = X + Y$$

it would be impossible to determine the value of Z since X and Y have no inherent values. If the following definitions in statements 10 and 20 were made:

$$10 \quad \text{LET } X = 5$$
$$20 \quad \text{LET } Y = 7$$
$$30 \quad \text{LET } Z = X + Y$$

the value of Z could be calculated because X and Y had been defined previously; Z is 12.

The following is also valid:

```
10  LET X = 1
20  LET Y = 14
30  LET Z = X + Y
```

Here again, the value of Z can be determined because the variables (X and Y) used in its computation have been defined.

Since the values X and Y are in fact variable, they may be defined, then used and changed if necessary. For example:

```
10  LET X = 10
20  LET Y = 15
30  LET Z = X + Y
40  ...
50  ...
60  LET Y = 3
70  LET Z = X + Y
```

Z, in the above example, takes on different values as the instructions are executed.

X, Y and Z are typical of variable names in BASIC.

RULES FOR NAMES

For numeric values in BASIC, a variable name is represented by a single letter or by a letter followed by a single digit. There are, therefore, 286 valid variable names in BASIC representing numeric data. Thus, the following are valid variable names.

A	B5
N	N1
K	D0
S	I9

Any variable name composed of more than a single alphabetic character or an alphabetic character followed by more than one digit is invalid. Thus, the following are invalid variable names.

```
AAA
NO12
10
NUM
```

If these rules are followed in selecting variable names, these names will be valid in all versions of BASIC. There are, however, some systems that allow a wider choice of variable names in that any two characters may be used. Some interpreters recognize two alphabetic characters and a numeric digit. Some permit the variable name to be any length but only look at the first two characters. Others allow longer variable names and use all the characters. Consult the documentation for your particular computer.

Variables are assigned values in the LET, FOR, READ and INPUT statements, which will be discussed in Chapters 4, 5 and 6.

NUMERIC DATA

The majority of processing in BASIC deals with the manipulation of numbers. These numbers can take the form of integers or fractional values in decimal form; they may be either positive or negative. Some examples of valid BASIC numbers are:

235	−.05
37.5	−235
3.001	0

Numbers such as these may appear in LET, FOR, PRINT and DATA statements.

Two examples of invalid numbers are:

$$2+3$$
$$32-$$

The first number contains a plus sign, which indicates an operation rather than a sign. The sign of the second number is improperly placed to the right of the number.

FLOATING-POINT NOTATION

The maximum number of digits that may be printed depends on the particular computer system. If the number to be printed exceeds the maximum allowable, the value will be printed in exponential form using floating-point notation. Thus the value 1000000 could be printed by the computer as

$$1E+6 \text{ or } 1E6$$

In this example, the 1 occupies the position known as the mantissa, and the 6 is in the position of the exponent. The expression 1E6 represents 1×10^6, or 1000000.

The number 25678000 could be represented by any one of the following:

$$256.78E5$$
$$25.678E6$$
$$.25678E8$$

All of these have the same value.

The exponent may be negative, indicating a fractional value. The following pairs of values are equivalent.

$$.00275 \quad = \quad 275E-5$$
$$.00000001 \quad = \quad 1E-8$$

A floating-point number may be negative, as shown by the following pairs of values.

$$-2.575 \quad = \quad -2575E-3$$
$$-.00025 \quad = \quad -25E-5$$

It is important to be aware that large numbers will be printed in this format. The programmer using BASIC must be able to recognize a value being represented in this fashion.

ALPHANUMERIC DATA

In addition to the numeric values mentioned, most programs also require that fields, such as descriptions, names, addresses and titles, be stored, compared or printed. These fields may contain numeric characters as well as alphabetic; for example, an address may have a street name and a house number.

The standard maximum size of an alphanumeric string is 132 characters; however, this may vary on some systems.

ALPHANUMERIC NAMES

Variable names for string data generally consist of an alphabetic character followed by a dollar sign. On some systems, a letter and a digit followed by a dollar sign are permissible. The following represent valid alphanumeric variable names:

```
A$        T$
Z$        H$
E$        N$
```

For some versions of BASIC, the following are also valid.

```
A1$
K3$
S7$
```

Test your system or check the documentation of your particular machine.

Alphanumeric data may be assigned to a variable through the LET, INPUT or READ statements. Such data may be assigned to another string variable, compared to another string value, or printed on an available output device.

Calculations with an alphanumeric field are not permissible. An action of this kind results in an error message and the termination of the program.

Chapter 4 explains further some of the uses of string data.

CHOOSING A VARIABLE NAME

When a variable name is chosen to represent a value, it is advisable to use a name that bears some resemblance to the value being stored. For example, to represent sales, the variable S might be used; C might represent a cost field; C1, C2 and C3 could be used as counters; N$ might represent a name and A$ an address. When confusion may result from the use of a variable name, a REM statement should be included to clarify its use.

This care in naming variables will pay large dividends in terms of readable and understandable programs.

QUESTIONS

1.   Why can there not be duplicate line numbers in a BASIC program?
2.   What is the reason for not incrementing line numbers by one?
3.   What is the difference between a keyword and a parameter?
4.   What effect do remarks have on a BASIC program?
5.   Identify the valid variable names in the following list:

a)	Z	**f)**	#6
b)	F7	**g)**	A0
c)	3	**h)**	READ
d)	IN	**i)**	AA
e)	TOTAL	**j)**	I$

6.   How can a valid decimal number be recognized?
7.   Which of the following are valid numbers in BASIC?

   a)   −46
   b)   640
   c)   71−
   d)   003
   e)   43+1

8.   What restriction is placed on the manipulation of alphanumeric data?
9.   What are the basic elements of each BASIC statement?
10.   What is the purpose of spacing in BASIC statements?
11.   What are the rules for numeric and alphanumeric variable names:
12.   Explain how floating-point numbers are represented.
13.   Represent the following values as floating-point numbers.
   a)   256
   b)   one billion
   c)   1000
   d)   92628

4
Arithmetic
and
String
Operations

Computers are machines that have the capacity to store data and instructions and the capability to perform complex mathematical computations very quickly. The BASIC command that allows the programmer to specify a calculation or an assignment is the LET statement. The following are typical LET commands:

```
10   LET B = 5
20   LET P = 3.14159
30   LET A = B + P
40   LET X = B - 9
```

The values of the variables B, P, A and X have been defined by these statements as follows:

```
B   is 5
P   is 3.14159
A   is 8.14159
X   is -4      (negative value)
```

Two important rules which have been illustrated in this example.

1.   The LET statement always assigns a value to a variable.

2.   The variable receiving the value must be shown to the left of the equal sign (=).

Therefore, the statement must always have the format shown in Figure 4.1.

statement number   LET   variable = { constant / variable / arithmetic expression }

FIGURE 4.1   LET Statement—General Format

In many BASIC systems, the keyword LET is optional. BASIC can operate on the data and assign a value properly without the keyword. This can be tested on your system or checked in the documentation for your particular machine. A statement written this way looks like this:

```
10   A = 4.74
```

The LET statement is a command, not an equation. A value is obtained from the specification to the right of the equal sign, and that value is placed in the variable on the left. It is important that this be remembered for a thorough understanding of the LET statement.

ASSIGNMENT OF DATA

The LET statement is represented in a flowchart by the process symbol. In some of the flowcharting examples in Chapter 2, there were process symbols at the beginning, showing that a counter or accumulator was to be set to zero or a variable set to 1. This is one use of the LET statement; the following statements might be seen in any BASIC program requiring variables for use as counters or accumulators.

```
10   LET C = 0
20   LET T1 = 1
30   LET T2 = 0
40   LET T3 = T1
```

The variables could now be used in the instructions that follow since the programmer is certain of their respective values, shown below:

```
C    is   0
T1   is   1
T2   is   0
T3   is   1
```

It should be noted that BASIC starts all variables with a value of zero at the beginning of each program. However, many programmers prefer to include a statement such as:

```
10   LET C1 = 0
```

in a program to document that this value is expected.

ARITHMETIC OPERATIONS

In the flowcharting examples in Chapter 2, process symbols were used to indicate calculations:

```
┌─────────────┐      ┌─────────────┐
│   ADD 1     │      │  CALCULATE  │
│    TO       │      │    THE      │
│  COUNTER    │      │  PRODUCT    │
└─────────────┘      └─────────────┘
```

+	Addition
−	Subtraction
*	Multiplication
/	Division
↑ or ** or ^	Exponentiation
	− depending on the system, one of these will be used.

FIGURE 4.2   Arithmetic Operators

The LET command is the BASIC statement that is used to specify such calculations. Figure 4.2 shows the arithmetic operators that may be used in the LET statement.

ADDITION

The statement

$$30 \quad \text{LET S} = 35 + 10$$

results in the value 45 being assigned to S. Likewise, in the command where the value of S is used:

$$120 \quad \text{LET X} = \text{S} + 7 + 8$$

the expression is evaluated, and the value 60 is assigned to X.

SUBTRACTION

In the command

$$40 \quad \text{LET D} = 12 - 7$$

D is given the value 5, the result of the subtract operation in the expression 12 − 7. The variable N would receive the value -14.5 in the following statement:

$$60 \quad \text{LET N} = \text{D} - 19.5$$

MULTIPLICATION

The symbol to indicate multiplication is the asterisk in the command

$$50 \quad \text{LET B} = 4 * 7$$

B is given the value 28. J is assigned the value 58.8 in the following statement:

$$75 \quad \text{LET } J = B * 2.1$$

DIVISION

The divide operation,

$$100 \quad \text{LET } X = 42/5$$

indicated by the slash, yields the quotient 8.4, which would be stored in X.

EXPONENTIATION

The word "exponentiation" is not as familiar to most people as the common arithmetic operations. However, it is an operation that is understood by most of us; it is the operation indicated by the small number at the upper right of another value.

$$3^2$$
$$5^3$$
$$X^n$$

The number in the corner is called the power or exponent. When we read it we say "three squared," "five cubed" or "X to the nth."
A LET command might read:

$$95 \quad \text{LET } T = 7 \uparrow 2$$

The value of T after this statement is executed is 49. In the statement

$$100 \quad \text{LET } V = 5 \uparrow 2.5$$

the value of V is 55.9017.
Some BASIC systems accept the command written with either the double asterisk or the caret, as indicated in Figure 4.2. Thus, the following two statements represent the same value.

$$95 \quad \text{LET } T = 7 ** 2$$
$$95 \quad \text{LET } T = 7 \char94 2$$

	symbol	
highest priority	(	)
	↑ **	∧
	*	/
lowest priority	+	−

FIGURE 4.3 Hierarchy of Arithmetic Operations

HIERARCHY OF OPERATIONS

The word "hierarchy" simply means priority. The need for a system of priorities becomes evident when several arithmetic operations are specified in one LET command. In the following statement

40 LET N = 6 + 4 * 2

which operation should be done first?

BASIC must have some rules that allow us to determine whether the value stored in N will be 20 (addition first) or 14 (multiplication first). Figure 4.3 illustrates the order of priority that BASIC gives to these operations. From Figure 4.3, two important observations should be made:

1. Brackets, or parentheses, have been included. They do not indicate any calculation, but may be used in pairs to show which operation is to be done first.

2. Multiplication and division share the same priority level, as do addition and subtraction. Operations of the same priority are executed from left to right.

With the priority levels defined, we see that the statement

40 LET N = 6 + 4 * 2

BASIC performs the multiplication first, and therefore the answer is 14.

Here is a more complex example.

```
50   LET Y = 3
60   LET Z = 4
70   LET T = 3
80   LET X = 9
90   LET A = Z * T − X/Y
```

In statement 90, three separate calculations specified are: multiplication, subtraction and division. The multiplication and division have the same priority; both are of higher priority than the subtraction. In determining the value assigned to the variable A, operations of the same priority are done from left to right; therefore, the evaluation takes place as follows:

1. Z * T: BASIC performs the multiplication to arrive at the answer 12 (4 * 3);

2. X / Y: The division results in a quotient of 3 (9/3);

3. 12 − 3: The subtraction is done using the results of the first two calculations, yielding a final answer 9, which is stored in A.

Consider this statement:

$$50 \quad \text{LET D3} = K\!\uparrow\!2 - X7\!\uparrow\!3/4.7$$

Even though the values used in the statement are not shown, we can still predict the sequence in which the operations will be performed. The sequence is shown here by numbering the operations in the order in which BASIC will evaluate them.

$$\begin{array}{ccccc} & (1) & (4) & (2) & (3) \\ 50 \quad \text{LET D3} = K\uparrow & 2 & - & X7\uparrow & 3 / 4.7 \end{array}$$

INCREMENTING A VARIABLE

One of the most interesting and useful features of the LET statement is that the variable on the left side of the equal sign may be used in the calculation on the right. The result is a new version of the particular variable whose value was used on the right to contribute toward the new value.

In Figure 4.4, the value originally given to C is zero. That value is printed by statement 20 and appears as the first amount printed by the program. The effect of statement 30 is to add 1 to the value of C, which increases its value to 1 (0 + 1), and to store this computed value in the variable on the left, C. The new value of C is printed after the first value by statement 40.

In Figure 4.5, X is assigned a value of 5 by statement 10. The value of X is reduced by 1 in each of statements 30, 50, 70, 90 and 110. Statements 40, 60, 80, 100 and 120 show the result of each reduction as the value of X goes from 5 to 0.

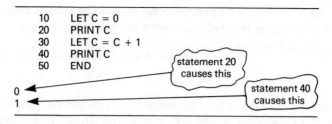

```
10    LET C = 0
20    PRINT C
30    LET C = C + 1
40    PRINT C
50    END
```

FIGURE 4.4   Incrementing a Variable

```
10    LET X = 5
20    PRINT X
30    LET X = X − 1
40    PRINT X
50    LET X = X − 1
60    PRINT X
70    LET X = X − 1
80    PRINT X
90    LET X = X − 1
100   PRINT X
110   LET X = X − 1
120   PRINT X
130   END
```

```
5
4
3
2
1
0
```

FIGURE 4.5   Decrementing a Variable

BRACKETS

When we first examined the BASIC statement

$$40 \quad \text{LET N} = 6 + 4 * 2$$

we discovered that BASIC assigns the value 14 to N since the multiplication is done first. By using brackets, the programmer can change the sequence in which BASIC evaluates the operations. This is done by writing the statement as follows:

$$40 \quad \text{LET N} = (6 + 4) * 2$$

The priorities have been altered by the use of brackets to cause the addition to be done first; thus, the value assigned to N is now 20.

Some formulas cannot be done in a single BASIC statement without the use of brackets. Consider the following formula:

$$r = \frac{a + b}{c / d}$$

This set of calculations requires brackets to indicate the sequence in which the evaluation should take place. The BASIC command that accomplishes this is:

10   LET R = (A + B)/(C/D)

Here is another formula:

$$n = \frac{s(a - p)}{2z}$$

The BASIC statement is:

10   LET N = S * (A − P) /(2 * Z)

SPACING

The following three statements are equivalent in many versions of BASIC.

```
10   LET T = 2 * 4
10LETT=2*4
10   LE   TT=   2*   4
```

In other words, spaces are not important in some BASIC systems. If, however, your BASIC system does not allow this flexibility, it is probably not a disadvantage. There is very little value in making programs difficult to read and understand.

MULTIPLE LET STATEMENT

On some extended BASIC systems, it is possible to assign a value to several variables at once.

10   LET A = B = C = 0

Each of the variables A, B and C is set to zero by the above command.

There is another format of the multiple LET statement that is valid for some BASIC systems. It is expressed as follows in order to achieve the same results.

$$10 \quad \text{LET A,B,C} = 0$$

The assignment of a multiple LET statement could also be the result of a calculation.

$$30 \quad \text{LET X} = \text{Y} = \text{Z} = 4 * 9 - 7$$

Example 1

The following statements are instructions in a BASIC program. The value stored in the variable is shown at the right.

```
10  LET X = 10          (10)
20  I = X - 3           (7)
30  J = X * I ↑ 2       (490)
40  K = J / 100         (4.9)
50  LET A = A + 1       (1)
60  LET M = M + A       (1)
```

COMMON ERRORS

One of the problems encountered when learning BASIC is that of recognizing that an error has been made and knowing how to correct it. These are some of the errors commonly made when coding the LET statement.

1.   10   LET 4 + 8 = A

The receiving variable must always be to the left of the equal sign. *Correction*: 10   LET A = 4 + 8

2.   S45   LET N = 4

Only numbers may be used in the statement number. *Correction*: 45   LET N = 4

3.   50   LET C = (K + 4)(M − 8)

There is no operation specified between the two sets of brackets. *Correction*: 0   LET C = (K + 4) * (M − 8)

4.   30   LET M = (C + 8) * 4)

Brackets must always be used in pairs. The last bracket is not necessary. *Correction*: 30   LET M = (C + 8) * 4

5.   150   LET NUM = 47

The variable names must fit BASIC's rules. NUM is not valid on most systems. *Correction*: 150   LET N=47

6.   90   LET X = A / * B

Two operations are specified. Which operation is required? *Correction*: 90   LET X = A / B

7.   20   LET A = 10,400

The comma is used to separate items in a BASIC program. *Correction*: 20   LET A = 10400

8.   25   LET D = $46.98

The dollar sign is a character, not a number. It must not be specified. *Correction*: 25   LET D = 46.98

9.   60   LET G = 75-

If a negative sign is required, it must precede the number. *Correction*: 60   LET G = −75

ALPHANUMERIC DATA

The manipulation of alphanumeric data (data composed of letters, numbers or special characters) is possible but is restricted in that no calculations may be performed on alphanumeric fields.

Unlike numbers, alphanumeric data must be enclosed in quotation marks denoting the beginning and end of what is known as the literal. The following program illustrates the assignment of a value to an alphanumeric variable, A$, and the subsequent printing of the variable.

```
10   LET A$="BANK BALANCE"
20   PRINT A$
30   END
```

BANK BALANCE

The alphanumeric value that has been assigned to one variable may be assigned to a second variable.

```
10   LET A$ = "OUTSTANDING CHECKS"
20   LET B$ = A$
30   PRINT B$
40   END
```

OUTSTANDING CHECKS

Both A$ and B$ contain the words OUTSTANDING CHECKS.

The typical use of alphanumeric literals and variables is for printing titles and explanatory remarks during program execution.

Example 2

Alphanumeric values are assigned to each of the following variable names. The resulting contents of each variable are shown at the right of each statement.

```
10  LET N$ = "NAME"      (NAME)
20  A$ = "ADDRESS"       (ADDRESS)
30  B$ = N$              (NAME)
```

ALPHANUMERIC OPERATIONS AND FUNCTIONS

Some BASIC systems have the capability to manipulate alphanumeric data by using powerful functions, some of which are mentioned in the following discussion. All versions of BASIC allow string comparisons, which are further discussed in Chapter 6.

The following is a summary of some of the string operations that may be available on your system. See Appendix F for other arithmetic and string functions.

CONCATENATION

Two string fields may be joined together by using the string operator "+". When used with alphanumeric data, the plus sign does not indicate addition, but rather that the fields are to be joined to form one long field. For example:

```
10  A$="SHELF"
20  B$="BOOK"
30  C$=B$+A$
40  PRINT C$
50  END
```

BOOKSHELF

STRING FUNCTIONS

Basic string functions include the following:

LEFT$(A$,N):   isolates the left-most N characters of A$.

40   LET B$=LEFT$("GREATEST",5)
50   PRINT B$

GREAT

LEN(A$):   provides the number of characters in the string A$.

10   LET D=LEN("NEVERNEVERLAND")
20   PRINT D

14

MID$(A$,S,N):   isolates the string, N characters long, starting at position S in the character string A$. If N is not specified, MID$ gives the string from S to the end (right-most character).

10   PRINT MID$("MICROCOMPUTER",6,7)
COMPUTE
10   PRINT MID$(MICROCOMPUTER",6)
COMPUTER

RIGHT$(A$,N):   isolates the right-most N characters of A$.

100   PRINT RIGHT$("ALPHANUMERIC",7)
NUMERIC

COMMON ERRORS

The following statements illustrate some of the common errors made in alphanumeric operations.

1.   5   LET A$ = "NEW BALANCE

The quotation mark begins the literal properly, but there is no closing quote. *Correction:* 5   LET A$ = "NEW BALANCE"

2.   155   LET M = "TOTAL"

The variable name to which the assignment is made is not a valid alphanumeric variable name.
Correction: 155   LET M$ = "TOTAL"

3.   70   LET J$ = A$ * N

An alphanumeric field may not be used in a calculation. No correction is possible. If calculations are necessary, numeric variables must be used.

4.   85   LET "NEXT DATA" = T$

The variable to which the assignment is made must always be on the left side of the equal sign.
Correction: 85   LET T$ = "NEXT DATA"

5.   C12   LET X$ = "QUESTION"

The statement number is valid.
Correction: 12   LET X$ = "QUESTION"

6.   120   LET K$ = TITLE

There are no quotation marks enclosing the word TITLE.
Correction: 120   LET K$ = "TITLE"

QUESTIONS

1.   In what order would the operations in the following statements be performed? Example:

$$\text{10   LET A} = \underset{(2)}{4} \overset{(1)}{*} (3 - 1) \underset{(4)}{+} 12 \underset{(3)}{/} 4$$

a)   100   M = 9 + 3 ↑ 3 * 2 - 20 /4

b)   140   LET Q = A ↑ (B + C) * 8 - D

c)   150   S = Z - Y + X

d)   160   G4 = G4 + T2 * 9 / K

e)   175   LET H1 = H1 + 2 * J + 16

2.   What value would be assigned to the variables in the following statements?

			Value
a)	50	LET N = 15 / 3	_____
b)	70	A$ = "QUESTION"	_____
c)	85	LET L = 3 + 5 * 7	_____
d)	90	I = 6 + 2 ↑ 3	_____
e)	100	Z = 17 - 4 * 3 ↑ 2 / 12 + 5	_____

3.   Write a LET statement for each of the following in order to assign the data to the associated variable.

	Variable	Data
a)	N	000.00
b)	K2	2.5
c)	T1	1010
d)	N$	JACK SMITH
e)	Z	.00001
f)	J	10^9

4.   Given the following assignments, show the result after each LET statement has been executed in the order shown.

_____   10 LET A = 1.0
_____   20 LET B = 2.0

```
_____    30 LET N = 4
_____    40 LET X = A + B
_____    50 Y = A * B
_____    60 Z = A / B
_____    70 LET W = X + Y − Z
_____    80 LET X = X * Y ↑ B / N
_____    90 C = Y ↑ B ↑ 2
_____    100 LET C = (Y ↑ B) ↑ 2
_____    110 LET D = ((( A * 2.0 * B) / N) ↑ 3) − 1.0
_____    120 LET K = −(N)
_____    130 LET N = −(K) * −(N)
```

5. Write a correct LET statement for each of the incorrect com-
    mands shown below.

		Incorrect	Correct
a)	10	LET A2 = 2,500	_____
b)	20	X$ = ERROR	_____
c)	S35	LET M = 5 * 3	_____
d)	50	LET A + B = C	_____
e)	100	XY = N + 1	_____
f)	125	H = (A + B)(C * D)	_____
g)	130	J = 6 / B + 2C	_____
h)	150	K = $599.98	_____
i)	155	LET "LINE" = L$	_____
j)	170	LET C = Z$ + B	_____

6. Each time a print is executed, we wish to add 2 to a LINE
    COUNT variable. Write a statement to accomplish this, using
    L as the counter variable.

7. Write equivalent BASIC statements for the following algebraic
    expressions ($\pi = 3.1416$).

a) $h = a \cdot b$

b) $a = b + c - d - e$

c) $c = \dfrac{a \cdot b}{e}$

d) $x = \dfrac{y + z}{w \cdot v}$

e) $j = \dfrac{k + (i/n)}{m}$

f) $r = \pi r^2$

g) $v = \dfrac{4 \pi r^3}{3}$

h) $a = \pi r \sqrt{r^2 + h^2}$

i) $e = a^{nj}$

j) $k = \sqrt{\dfrac{x + y}{z}}$

k) $y = \sqrt{x^n}$

l) $h = \sqrt{R^2 - r^2}$

m) $x = \dfrac{-b + \sqrt{b^2 - 4ac}}{2a}$

8.   Write BASIC statements to compute the area and the circumference of a circle of given radius.

$$A = \pi r^2$$
$$C = 2\pi r$$

9.   The formulas to compute the volume and surface area of a sphere of given radius are shown below. Write BASIC statements to compute the two values.

$$A = 4\pi r^2$$
$$V = \frac{3}{4}\pi r^3$$

10.   The economic order quantity for a part is given by the formula:

$$EOQ = \sqrt{\frac{2dc}{us}}$$

where   d is the demand in units for a given time period, c is the cost of placing an order, u is the unit cost of the part, and s is the cost of storing the item in stock. Write the BASIC statement to calculate the EOQ.

5
Data
Input
and
Output

PRINT

The PRINT statement allows us to display the results of program execution. On many systems, it is the only method of creating output. Figure 5.1 shows the general format of the PRINT statement.

At this point, we will look at the PRINT statement in its elementary form. Later in the chapter, we will cover the advanced PRINT options, which are available on many BASIC systems.

statement number	PRINT	data list – consisting of one or more constants, variables, expressions, alphanumeric literals

FIGURE 5.1   PRINT statement—General Format

PRINT ZONES

For printed output on most BASIC systems, the page (or screen if CRT) is divided into five print zones. There are approximately 15 spaces, or print positions, in each print zone; the exact number depends on the particular computer system.

Figure 5.2 illustrates the typical format of a page. As values appear in the PRINT statement, they are printed on the page, the first in zone 1, the second in zone 2, etc. If 6 or more values are specified in one PRINT statement, the 6th is printed in zone 1 under the first, the 7th in zone 2 under the second, until all values have been printed. The data are printed at the left side of the PRINT zone.

PRINT EXAMPLES

Example 1:   *Printing the Contents of a Variable*

```
10  LET N = 4.95
20  PRINT N
30  END
```

4.95

Example 2:   *Printing Three Variables*

```
10  LET A = 7
20  LET B = 5
30  LET C = A * B
```

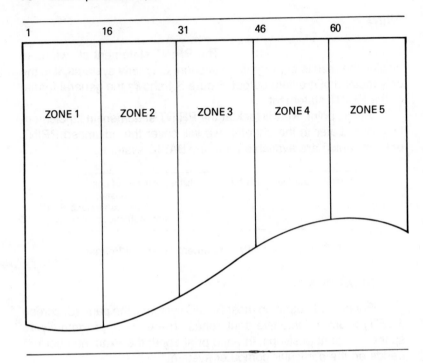

1	16	31	46	60
ZONE 1	ZONE 2	ZONE 3	ZONE 4	ZONE 5

FIGURE 5.2   PRINT Zones

```
40   PRINT A,B,C
50   END
```

7   5   35

Example 3: ***Printing the Result of a Calculation***

```
10   PRINT 3 * 2 ↑ 2
20   END
```

12

Example 4: ***Printing a Constant***

```
10   PRINT 47
20   END
```

47

Example 5: **Printing an Alphanumeric Literal**

```
10   PRINT "THIS IS A TEST"
20   END
```

THIS IS A TEST

Example 6: **Printing a "Heading" or Title and a "Detail" Line**

```
10   LET I = 4
20   LET J = 9
30   PRINT "NUMBER 1", "NUMBER 2", "PRODUCT"
40   PRINT I,J,I * J
50   END
```

NUMBER 1	NUMBER 2	PRODUCT
4	9	36

Example 7: **An Alphanumeric Literal and the Result of a Calculation**

```
10   PRINT "2 TO THE POWER OF 7 IS",2 ↑ 7
20   END
```

2 TO THE POWER OF 7 IS   128

Example 8: **Alphanumeric Literals and Variables**

```
10   M = 3.4
20   N = 2
30   PRINT "M=",M, "N=",N
40   END
```

M=   3.4   N=   2

Example 9: **Six Items in One PRINT Statement**

```
10   PRINT "HERE","ARE","SIX","PRINTED","DATA","ITEMS"
20   END
```

HERE   ARE   SIX   PRINTED   DATA
ITEMS

Example 10: Skip a Line

```
10  PRINT "THIS PRINTS ON LINE1"
20  PRINT
30  PRINT "THIS PRINTS ON LINE 3"
40  PRINT
50  PRINT
60  PRINT "THIS PRINTS ON LINE 6"
70  PRINT "TO PROVIDE DOUBLE OR TRIPLE SPACING"
80  END
```

THIS PRINTS ON LINE 1

THIS PRINTS ON LINE 3

THIS PRINTS ON LINE 6
TO PROVIDE DOUBLE OR TRIPLE SPACING

PRINTING IN SELECTED PRINT ZONES

It may be useful in some cases for data to appear in the first and third or the second and fifth PRINT zones with nothing printed in the unused zones. One of the following methods may be used to accomplish this. Notice that an additional comma (on some systems) simply indicates that a PRINT zone is to be skipped; it has the same effect as printing a blank in a PRINT zone.

Example 11

```
10  PRINT "FIRST"," ","THIRD"
20  END
```

FIRST   THIRD

Example 12

```
10  PRINT "FIRST",,"THIRD"
20  END
```

FIRST   THIRD

Example 13

```
10  PRINT " ", "SECOND", " "," ","FIFTH"
20  END
```

          SECOND   FIFTH

Example 14

```
10   PRINT , "SECOND",,,"FIFTH"
20   END
```

SECOND   FIFTH

COMMON ERRORS

The following statements illustrate some of the errors commonly made in writing PRINT statements.

1.   50   PRINT THE ANSWER IS, A

The alphanumeric literal must be enclosed by quotation marks. *Correction:* 50   PRINT "THE ANSWER IS",A

2.   75   PRINT "TOTAL SALES

Quotation marks must be used in pairs.
Correction: 75   PRINT "TOTAL SALES"

3.   100   PRINT "THE ANSWER IS,A"

Only the words to be printed should be enclosed by the quotation marks. *Correction:* 100   PRINT "THE ANSWER IS",A

4.   125   PRINT ABC

If this is to be printed as it is, it must be enclosed by quotation marks "ABC". If these are three variables to be printed, there must be commas between the variable names.
Correction: 125   PRINT A,B,C

5.   150   PRINT A B C

Commas must separate variables.
Correction: 150   PRINT A,B,C

6.   175   PRINT A$ * B$

Alphanumeric data may not be used in a calculation. If a calculation is required, use valid variable names.
Correction: 175   PRINT A * B

7.   PRINT P,R

All statements must have statement numbers.
Correction: 200   PRINT P,R

THE SEMICOLON

The commas used to separate the variables or values to be printed by the PRINT statement indicate that the next value is to appear at the beginning of the next PRINT zone. In some cases, the output would be more readable if the values were printed closer together. To give the programmer the option of closely spaced printing, BASIC permits the use of a semicolon to separate data items. Depending on the system involved, there are no or very few spaces left. The comma and semicolon may be used in the same PRINT statement to condense some data items and to separate others.

Example 15

```
10   PRINT "3 TO THE POWER OF 2 IS ";3 ↑ 2
20   END
```

3 TO THE POWER OF 2 IS 9

Example 16

```
10   LET A = 52
20   LET B = 10
30   PRINT "A=";A,"B=";B
40   END
```

A= 52   B= 10

On some BASIC systems, which leave no spaces between data values when the semicolon is used, it is necessary to leave an extra space at the end of an alphanumeric literal when the data to be printed next are also alphanumeric.

Example 17:   *No Space Between Printed Fields*

```
10   LET A$ = "JOHN SMITH"
20   PRINT "MY NAME IS";A$
30   END
```

MY NAME ISJOHN SMITH

Example 18:   *One Space Separating Fields*

```
10   LET A$ = "JOHN SMITH"
20   PRINT "MY NAME IS ";A$
30   END
```

MY NAME IS JOHN SMITH

The difference between Examples 17 and 18 is that in statement 20 a blank was placed within the quotation marks to make the output readable.

MULTIPLE PRINTS ON ONE LINE

Either the comma or the semicolon may be used at the end of a PRINT statement to suppress a line feed. This function is illustrated in the following two examples:

Example 19:   Five Lines Printed

```
10  PRINT "ITEM 1"
20  PRINT "ITEM 2"
30  PRINT "ITEM 3"
40  PRINT "ITEM 4"
50  PRINT "ITEM 5"
60  END
```

```
ITEM 1
ITEM 2
ITEM 3
ITEM 4
ITEM 5
```

If a comma is placed at the end of statements 10, 20 and 40, the line feed is suppressed, and the output is as shown in Example 20.

Example 20:   Two Lines Printed

```
10  PRINT "ITEM 1",
20  PRINT "ITEM 2",
30  PRINT "ITEM 3"
40  PRINT "ITEM 4",
50  PRINT "ITEM 5"
60  END
```

```
ITEM 1     ITEM 2     ITEM 3
ITEM 4     ITEM 5
```

The semicolon may be used to cause the suppression of line feed if the data is to be printed close together without regard to the print zones.

Example 21

```
10  PRINT "ITEM 1";
20  PRINT "ITEM 2";
30  PRINT "ITEM 3"
40  PRINT "ITEM 4";
50  PRINT "ITEM 5"
60  END

ITEM 1ITEM 2ITEM 3
ITEM 4ITEM 5
```

INPUT

The LET statement discussed in Chapter 5 allows a value to be assigned to a variable, which can then be used in the program. This is acceptable for a program that is intended for a specific purpose where the data values are known when the program is written and not subject to change if the program is to be run at a later date.

INPUT FROM KEYBOARD

The INPUT and the READ—DATA statements allow the facility of supplying a value to a variable or set of variables when the program is actually run. This feature can cause the results of program execution to vary since different values can be given each time the program is run.

The general format of the INPUT statement is shown in Figure 5.3. The execution of an INPUT statement causes two occurrences:

1. A question mark (?) is printed, requesting that data be typed.

2. The program pauses, allowing the entry of the required values from the keyboard.

---

statement number   INPUT   one or more variables

FIGURE 5.3   INPUT Statement—General Format

Example 22

```
10  INPUT N
20  PRINT "THE NUMBER TYPED WAS",N
30  END

? 32
THE NUMBER TYPED WAS        32
```

The only indication that a value was expected was the question mark. There was, in this case, no specification as to how many values or the type of data (number or string) expected. In such a case, the operator would have to know the program in order to be able to key in the proper data. To assist the operator, the program should provide instructions just before the input data is to be typed.

Example 23

```
10   PRINT "TYPE IN 2 NUMBERS"
20   INPUT A,B
30   LET C = A + B
40   PRINT "THE SUM OF";A;"AND";B;"IS";C
50   END
```

```
TYPE IN 2 NUMBERS
? 6,9
THE SUM OF 6 AND 9 IS 15
```

Alphanumeric data may also be entered from the keyboard, but the data must be enclosed in quotation marks on many systems.

Example 24

```
10   PRINT "TYPE IN THE DESCRIPTION AND COST"
20   INPUT A$,C
30   PRINT A$,C
40   END
```

```
TYPE IN THE DESCRIPTION AND COST
? "TABLE",59.95
TABLE          59.95
```

The question mark will be printed on the same line as the directions by ending the PRINT statement with a semicolon.

Example 25

```
10   PRINT "PLEASE ENTER THE NAME OF A MONTH";
20   INPUT M$
30   PRINT "YOU CHOSE THE MONTH ";M$
40   END
```

```
PLEASE ENTER THE NAME OF A MONTH? "JANUARY"
YOU CHOSE THE MONTH JANUARY
```

COMMON ERRORS

Here are some examples of errors that are common in using the INPUT statement.

1.   10   INPUT N M

Variable names must be separated by commas.
Correction: 10   INPUT N,M

2.   20   INPUT N,M
      ?3 4

Commas are also necessary between values when more than one value is entered to satisfy the requirements of an INPUT statement.
Correction: 20   INPUT N,M
                 ?3,4

3.   30   INPUT D$
      ?JULY 1, 1867

On some systems string values must be enclosed in quotation marks. In this case, it is necessary to use the quotation marks even if not required by the system because of the comma that forms part of the data.
Correction: 30   INPUT D$
                 ?"JULY 1,1867"

4.   40   INPUT K,L,M
      ?525
      ?

There are three variable names to receive values as a result of the INPUT statement, but only one value has been entered. In most systems, another question mark is typed, indicating that more data are required. *Correction:* Type in the proper number of values.

5.   50   INPUT X
      ?12,7

Too much data have been typed. This causes an error on some systems but is ignored on others. *Correction:* Again, type in the proper number of values.

6.   INPUT N,A$
      ?"NEW BALANCE",42.55

The data have been typed, but in the wrong sequence. *Correction:* Type in the data properly.

In many of the errors illustrated above, the error could have been avoided by printing instructions just before the INPUT statement. An INPUT should never be used by itself in a program but should follow a PRINT statement that explains the type and quantity of data required.

READ—DATA

The READ statement may be used to assign values to variables in a BASIC program. When the READ statement is used for this purpose, there must also be a DATA statement that supplies the values to the variables. The general format of the READ and DATA statements is shown in Figure 5.4.

statement number	READ	one or more variables
statement number	DATA	one or more constants

FIGURE 5.4   READ and DATA Statements—General Format

READ—DATA EXAMPLES

Example 26

When a READ statement is executed, each variable listed in the statement is assigned a value, which is taken from the constants in the DATA statement(s). The first variable is assigned the first value, the second variable takes the second value, and so on in order until all variables have been assigned values.

```
10   READ A,B,C
20   PRINT A,B,C
30   DATA 10,20,30
40   END
```

```
10          20          30
```

Example 27

The values may come from one DATA statement or may be assigned to the variables in the READ statement from several DATA statements.

```
10  READ A,B,C
20  PRINT A,B,C
30  DATA 10
40  DATA 20,30
50  END
```

```
10        20        30
```

Example 28

If there is not sufficient data to provide a value for each variable listed in the READ statement, a message is printed by the system to indicate the error. The exact wording of the error message depends on the particular system, but the following is typical of such a message.

```
LINE 180:  OUT OF DATA
```

```
10  READ A,B,C
20  PRINT A,B,C
30  DATA 10,20
40  END
```

```
LINE 10:  OUT OF DATA
```

Example 29

The READ statement may not "use up" all the data at one time. When all the variables have been assigned values, processing proceeds to the next instruction. A subsequent READ statement would continue from the point where the first one left off.

```
10   READ A,B
20   LET C = A + B
30   PRINT A;"+";B;"IS EQUAL TO";C
40   READ A,B
50   LET C = A + B
60   PRINT A;"+";B;"IS EQUAL TO";C
70   DATA 6
80   DATA 11
90   DATA 4
100  DATA 8
110  END
```

```
6 + 11 IS EQUAL TO   17
4 + 8 IS EQUAL TO   12
```

Example 30

Alphanumeric values may also be assigned by the READ statement. On some systems, the string data must be enclosed by quotation marks.

```
10  READ D$
20  PRINT "THE DATE IS ",D$
30  DATA "JULY 4, 1776"
40  END
```

THE DATE IS   JULY 4, 1776

Example 31

In the previous examples, the DATA statements have appeared just before the END statement, after all the other instructions. Although this is an acceptable practice in terms of program organization, it is not a rule that must be followed. The DATA statements may appear at any point in the program: before any of the other commands, in the middle of the program, or even scattered throughout the program. However, the END statement must be the last statement of any program.

```
10  DATA 100
20  READ A,B,C$
30  DATA 150
40  PRINT A,B,C$
50  DATA "ARE TWO NUMBERS"
60  END
```

100   150   ARE TWO NUMBERS

Example 32

```
10  DATA "SALE VALUE",1600,"DISCOUNT",160
20  READ S$,S
30  PRINT S$,S
40  READ D$,D
50  PRINT D$,D
60  PRINT "NET SALE",S − D
70  END
```

SALE VALUE   1600
DISCOUNT   160
NET SALE   1440

One DATA statement may contain more values than one READ statement requires. The remaining values are available, as required, to successive READ statements.

Example 33

The values in the DATA statement may be negative.

```
10  READ D,E
20  J = D * E
30  PRINT D,E,J
40  DATA 6,−4
50  END
```

```
6           −4          −24
```

RESTORE

The RESTORE statement, available on many BASIC systems, specifies that the values in DATA statements are to be made available to the READ statement from the beginning. In other words, it allows the program to reread the data.

Example 34

```
10  READ A,B
20  PRINT A,B
30  RESTORE
40  READ X,Y,Z
50  PRINT X,Y,Z
60  DATA 3,7,10
70  END
```

```
3           7
3           7           10
```

In example 34, the values assigned by the READ statements were:

```
Line 10:    A=3
            B=7
Line 40:    X=3
            Y=7
            Z=10
```

COMMON ERRORS

The following examples illustrate some of the common errors made in coding READ—DATA statements.

1.  ```
    10   READ N,M
    20   DATA 6
    30   PRINT N,M
    40   END
    ```
    LINE 10: OUT OF DATA

    There is insufficient data to supply values to both variables in the READ statement. The program could not proceed. *Correction:* 20   DATA 6,8

2.  ```
    10   READ A$,B
    20   DATA 45,"ANSWER"
    ```

    The first variable in the READ statement is alphanumeric, the second is numeric. The values in the DATA statement are the reverse. *Correction:* 20 DATA "ANSWER",45

3.  ```
    10   DATA 3,4
    20   READ A,B,
    ```

    The extra comma after B in line 20 may cause an error on some systems. *Correction:* 20   READ A,B

4.  ```
    10   READ N,N$
    20   17,"ACCOUNTS"
    ```

    The keyword DATA is missing from line 20. *Correction:* 20   DATA 17, "ACCOUNTS"

5.  ```
    10   READ A
    20   DATA 25,000
    ```

    The value 25,000, if it is one value, must not contain a comma. If it is not one value, then there is more data available than required. The variable A will be assigned the value 25. *Correction:* 20   DATA 25000

ADVANCED PRINT OPTIONS

On many BASIC systems, it is possible to gain even greater control over the way values are printed than by simply using the comma or the semicolon. The TAB option specifies that a value is to
    ```

begin in a certain print position, much like the TAB function on a typewriter. The image statement allows the user to type in a line in the format in which it is to be printed so that the number of spaces and the alignment of columns is directly controlled.

TAB

The TAB option is used in the PRINT command to cause printing to begin at a particular print position. It could be used as follows:

40   PRINT TAB(10);A;TAB(19);B;TAB(32);"TEST"

In this example, the value of A would be printed starting at print position 10. When numeric values are printed, a space is provided at the left side of the number to allow for a possible negative sign; therefore, the first digit of A will appear in column 11. Likewise, the value of B would be printed starting at position 19, with the first digit in column 20 and column 19 indicating a sign if B is negative. The literal value "TEST" would begin at column 32, with no space provided, since it is an alphanumeric data item.

In some of the following examples, a line of numbers is printed to illustrate the print positions used. Note that, for most versions of BASIC, the first position is called 0, not 1; this may not be the case on your particular system.

Example 35

```
10 PRINT "01234567890123456789012345678901234567890123456789"
20 READ A,B$,C
30 PRINT TAB(8);A;TAB(20);B$;TAB(27);C
40 DATA 1,COUNT,2
50 END

01234567890123456789012345678901234567890123456789
        1           COUNT     2
```

The value specified in the TAB option may also be a variable.

Example 36

```
10 PRINT "TYPE IN THE COLUMN NUMBER,"
20 PRINT "AND THE NUMBER TO BE PRINTED";
30 INPUT A,B
40 PRINT "01234567890123456789012345678901234567890123456789"
50 PRINT TAB(A);B
60 END

TYPE IN THE COLUMN NUMBER,
AND THE NUMBER TO BE PRINTED ? 20,-475
01234567890123456789012345678901234567890123456789
                    -475
```

PRINT USING AND IMAGE STATEMENTS

The PRINT USING statement together with the *image* statement may be used to control the spacing of printed data. This feature allows precise control of the output, which is not available with the use of print zones and semicolons. The general format is shown in Figure 5.5.

The key to the PRINT USING statement is the related image statement. It is this statement, identified by the statement number in the PRINT USING statement, that defines how the output data are to appear on the printed line. The image statement may contain alphanumeric data, such as a heading, or it may include specific image characters, which identify the type of data to be printed and their position in the line. These image characters are described in Figure 5.6.

The image statement contains no keyword, such as READ, LET or IF, but is identified by a colon (:), which follows its statement number.

---

statement number   PRINT USING   statement number, data list

statement number: image

FIGURE 5.5   PRINT USING and image—General Format

#	This character represents the print position for a numeric digit. One # is required for each digit.
	A period shows the position of the decimal point in a numeric field.
$	If a numeric field represents dollars and cents, a dollar sign may be placed at the left side of the field.
↑↑↑↑	These arrows represent the four positions to be occupied by the E notation used for exponential values.
'	An apostrophe is used to indicate the first print position of a character string. This is normally followed by one of the image characters, L, R, C or E, and counts as one of the characters of the string.
L	This image character indicates that a character string (alphanumeric data item) is to be left-adjusted in the field of L's.
R	A character string is to be right-adjusted in the field.
C	A character string is to be centered in the field.
E	The field is to be left-adjusted and extended on the right by sufficient print positions to accomodate the entire length of the string.

FIGURE 5.6   Image Characters

NOTES ON FIGURE 5.6. These symbols are representative oɪ most BASIC systems. However, some systems may substitute different symbols to obtain the same results.

Any other symbol appearing in the image represents a character that is to be printed as is. A heading or other description could therefore be printed.

Example 37

The first print position immediately follows the colon. The output for the image in Example 1 is printed in columns 3, 4 and 5 (remember column 0). Column 3 is blank because the value printed is 35 and does not require the hundreds position.

```
00010   A=35
00020   PRINT USING 30,A
00030:  ###
00040   END

        35
```

Example 38

If the value is fractional, e.g., dollars and cents, a decimal point may be included in the image.

```
00010   A=365.85
00020   PRINT USING 30,A
00030:  ###.##
00040   END

        365.85
```

Example 39

Multiple images may be combined in one image statement, providing for spacing between the fields. The number of spaces between the images specifies the number of spaces between the fields on output.

```
00010   A1=35
00020   A2=365.85
00030   PRINT USING 40,A1,A2
00040:  ###   ###.##
```

```
00050   END
```

```
            35      365.85
```

Example 40

In this example, a floating dollar sign is used to cause the dollar sign to appear beside the left-most digit of the number. The unused positions on the left are blank filled.

```
00010   N=27.50
00020   PRINT USING 30,N
00030:  $####.##
00040   END
```

```
            $   27.50
```

Example 41

For scientific notation, the exponent may be specified in the image statement. In this example, the value of K is printed twice: the first time with four digits, of which two are decimal, and the second time with two digits, one of which is a decimal position.

```
00010   K=5638000000
00020   PRINT USING 30,K.K
00030:  ##.##↑↑↑↑  #.#↑↑↑↑
00040   END
```

```
      56.38E+08      5.6E+09
```

Example 42

Character strings may be manipulated easily, as illustrated here. The last three lines of output show the use of the L, R, C and E

```
010 A$="LEFT"
020 B$="RIGHT"
030 C$="CENTER"
040 D$="IMAGE STATEMENT IN EXTENDED BASIC"
050 PRINT "01234567890123456789012345678901234567889"
060 PRINT USING 70,A$,B$,C$
070:'LLLLLL'RRRRRR'CCCCCCCCCCCCC
080 PRINT USING 90,D$
090:'E
100 PRINT USING 110,
110:MAY BE USED FOR HEADINGS OR DESCRIPTIONS
120 END

01234567890123456789012345678901234567889
LEFT     RIGHT    CENTER
IMAGE STATEMENT IN EXTENDED BASIC
MAY BE USED FOR HEADINGS OR DESCRIPTIONS
```

codes as well as the direct printing of an image with no codes. The comma in statement 100 may not be required by all BASIC systems.

The following programs illustrate the use of the PRINT USING statement to align columns under headings. Also shown is the printing of digits to the right of a decimal point, such as 0.10 to represent 10 cents. Without the PRINT USING statement, this would appear as 0.1.

Example 43

The following program does not use the PRINT USING statement.

```
010 PRINT "ID NO.","AMOUNT","DISCOUNT","NET AMOUNT"
020 READ I,A,D
030 IF I=9999 THEN 90
040 N=A-(A*D)
050 T1=T1+A
060 T2=T2+N
070 PRINT I,A,D,N
080 GO TO 20
090 PRINT ,T1,,T2
100 PRINT
110 PRINT "END OF PROGRAM"
120 DATA 1234,245.50,.10
130 DATA 2345,10.65,.07
140 DATA 3456,9.00,.15
150 DATA 4567,70.00,.20
160 DATA 5678,50.00,.25
170 DATA 6789,40.98,.30
180 DATA 9999,9,9
190 END
```

ID NO.	AMOUNT	DISCOUNT	NET AMOUNT
1234	245.5	0.1	220.95
2345	10.65	0.07	9.9045
3456	9	0.15	7.65
4567	70	0.2	56
5678	50	0.25	37.5
6789	40.98	0.3	28.686
	426.13		360.6905

END OF PROGRAM

Even though the answers are, strictly speaking, correct, the output is not consistent. For example, the amount $245.50 is printed as 245.5; and $9.00 is printed simply as 9. In the NET AMOUNT column, 9.9045 is the result after a discount of 0.07 has been applied to $10.65, and the total at the bottom is $360.6905. These figures are correct, but not useful in representing dollars and cents. The columns of figures are aligned on the left rather than the right, as might be expected with numeric data.

Example 44

In the following program, the PRINT USING statement is used to control the printing of the data. The headings appear in the normal print zones.

The alignment of fields is handled by the images, ensuring that a variable always occupies the same print position regardless of its value. Dollar figures are always printed with two decimal positions and are aligned on the right. All this makes the report easier to read.

```
010 PRINT "ID NO.","AMOUNT","DISCOUNT","NET AMOUNT"
020 READ I,A,D
030 IF I=9999 THEN 100
040 N=A-(A*D)
050 T1=T1+A
060 T2=T2+N
070 PRINT USING 80,I,A,D,N
080: ####        ###.##        #.##        ####.##
090 GO TO 20
100 PRINT USING 110,T1,T2
110:            ####.##                    ####.##
120 PRINT
130 PRINT "END OF PROGRAM"
140 DATA 1234,245.50,.10
150 DATA 2345,10.65,.07
160 DATA 3456,9.00,.15
170 DATA 4567,70.00,.20
180 DATA 5678,50.00,.25
190 DATA 6789,40.98,.30
200 DATA 9999,9,9
310 END
```

ID NO.	AMOUNT	DISCOUNT	NET AMOUNT
1234	245.50	0.10	220.95
2345	10.65	0.07	9.90
3456	9.00	0.15	7.65
4567	70.00	0.20	56.00
5678	50.00	0.25	37.50
6789	40.98	0.30	28.69
	426.13		360.69

END OF PROGRAM

COMMON ERRORS

1.
```
10  READ A$
20  PRINT "THE ANSWER TO QUESTION 7 IS";TAB(8);A$
30  DATA CORRECT
40  END
```
THE ANSWER TO QUESTION 7 ISCORRECT

The TAB is ignored since the specified print position has already been passed.

2.
```
10  X=4
20  Y=7
30  PRINT X,TAB(8),Y
40  END
```
4   7

Here too, the TAB does not take effect since the comma after X in line 30 indicates an advance to the next print zone, well past the TAB value.

3. 10 PRINT USING 20,A,B
    20   ###   ###

The image statement has no colon and is therefore not recognizable. *Correction:* 20:   ### ###

4. 50 PRINT USING 60,A$,B$
    60:    LLLLL   RRRRR

There is no apostrophe at the beginning of the image characters. *Correction:* If each image is to control five print positions, statement 60 should appear as follows:

                60:      'LLLL   'RRRR

QUESTIONS

1.   Write a PRINT statement to accomplish each of the following.

a)   Print the words THIS IS A SENTENCE.

b)   The amount is A, and the commission is C. Print the two values.

c)   Print the result of the calculation 4 * 8 ↑ 2.

d)   Print NUMBER ONE in zone 1, NUMBER TWO in zone 3.

e)   Print the value of N in zone 3 and of M in zone 5.

f)   Print the values of A1, A2, A3, A4, A5, and A6 on one line.

g)   Print the value of the string S$ followed as closely as possible by the numeric value S.

2.   Correct the errors in each of the following PRINT statements.

a)   N   PRINT M,P

b)   145   PRINT DAY,K

c)   155   PRINT REPORT"

d)   165   PRINT Z Y

e)   475   PRINT "THE VALUE OF A",IS;A

f)   585   PRINT 3 ↑ 4,47 - 18,D$ + 4,N * 7

3.   What will be printed by each of the following programs?

a)   10 M = 3
       20 N = 7
       30 PRINT N,M
       40 END

b)   10 X = 4
       20 Y = 5
       30 PRINT "X Y"," ",X,Y
       40 END

c)   10 LET A = 10
       20 LET B = 20
       30 LET C = 30
       40 PRINT C / (B / A)
       50 END

d)   10 LET A = 10
       20 LET B = -20

```
30  LET C = 30
40  PRINT "C =";C,"A ="; A,"B =";B
50  END
```

4. When commas are used to separate data values in the PRINT statement, how many values can be printed on one line?

5. Write two PRINT statements to write the values of A, B, C, D, E and F on one line such that A, B and C are grouped at the beginning of the line and D, E and F are grouped farther along on the line.

6. Write a program that assigns any two values to A and B. Print the values of A and B on one line, and print the sum and the product on the next line.

INPUT

1. What is the purpose of the INPUT statement?

2. What type and how many values are expected by each of the following INPUT statements?

    a) 10 INPUT A,B,C
    b) 30 INPUT Z$,T,C$
    c) 60 INPUT X,Y,Y$
    d) 80 INPUT N$,C,K,Q,M$

3. Supply INPUT statements that might have been used to accept each of the following responses.

    a) "DISTANCE",400
    b) "DEBIT",689.15,"CREDIT",12.48
    c. 1624,19.45,1010,3.25
    d) "DATE","TIME","LOCATION"

4. Identify any errors or discrepancies in the following sets of statements.

    a) 10 PRINT "TYPE IN 3 NUMBERS"
        20 INPUT A,B
    b) 100 PRINT "WHAT IS YOUR NAME"
        110 INPUT N
    c) 190 PRINT "TYPE IN ACCOUNT AND BALANCE"
        200 INPUT A,N$
    d) 250 INPUT X,Y
        260 PRINT "TYPE IN 2 NUMBERS"

5. Write the statements necessary to instruct that a number is

required from the keyboard, to accept the value, and to print the number that was entered.

6. Write the statements that will ask for and accept two numbers, calculate the sum, product, difference and quotient. Print the two numbers on one line, and the calculated values on the next.

READ—DATA

1. Write READ and DATA statements that will assign the following values.

    a)   52 to A; 71 to B; "ALPHA" to C$.

    b)   The name is SMITH; his salary is $30,000.

    c)   Sales are $1,400,000; commission is 10% (0.10).

    d)   A building is 14 stories high; there are 12 apartments on each floor.

2. Correct the errors in each of the following statements.

    a)   10   READ N$
             20   DATA 14

    b)   30   READ N
             40   DATA M

    c)   60   DATA 491
             70   READ A,B

    d)   15   READ K$,L$,M$
             16   DATA 1,2,3

    e)   5   READ Z,Y
             10   DATA 31 16

3. What will be printed by each of the following sets of statements?

    a)   100   READ X,Y,Z
             200   W = S + Y − Z
             300   PRINT W
             400   DATA 3
             500   DATA 4
             600   DATA 5
             700   END

    b)   10   DATA "DAY"
             20   DATA 1,2,3
             30   READ A$,I,J,K
             40   PRINT A$,I

```
        50   PRINT A$,J
        60   PRINT A$,K
        70   END
```

c)
```
        10   LET N = 10
        20   READ C
        30   N = N + C
        40   PRINT "N",N,"C",C
        50   DATA 7
        60   END
```

d)
```
         5   READ P,I
        10   S = (P * I) + P
        15   DATA 100,.08
        20   PRINT S
        25   END
```

4.   Read a 3-digit number (100 - 999), and print the number and its square.

5.   Read three 1-digit numbers (1 - 9). These are the dimensions in feet of a box. Calculate and print the volume of the box in cubic inches and the total area of all of its sides.

6.   The formula for the area of a triangle is ½bh, where b is the length of the base and h is the height. Read the base and height of a triangle, and determine its area. Print the dimensions and the area.

7.   The formula for compound interest is $P(1 + i)^n$, where P is the principal (amount), i is the interest rate and n is the number of years. In BASIC, this could be represented as P * (1 + I) ↑ N. Read in values for P, I and N and determine the value of an investment (P) at a certain interest rate (I) after a period of years (N). Note: 8% is 0.08. Print all the values, P, I and N, and the final value of the investment.

ADVANCED PRINT OPTIONS

1.   Correct the errors in each of the following.

a)   `10   PRINT "test",TAB(8),"RUN"`

b)   `30   PRINT USING 40,A,B`
`        40      ###  ###`

c)   `20   PRINT "DATA DESCRIPTION";TAB(6);A$`

d)   `80   PRINT A;TAB(6);B;TAB(6);C`

e)   `60   PRINT USING 70,A$`
`        70:        LLLLLLLLLL`

2. Write PRINT statements to satisfy each of the following requirements.

    a) Print the values of A, B and C, beginning in columns 10, 20 and 30, respectively. Use the TAB function.

    b) Repeat part a, but use the PRINT USING statement.

    c) Print the following heading:

```
PART        DESCRIPTION   QUANTITY   UNIT    EXTENDED
NUMBER                                COST    COST
```

    d) Align the variables P (part number), D$ (description), Q (quantity), C (unit cost) and E (extended cost) under the headings in part c. Use the PRINT USING statement.

3. In the printer spacing sheets provided, show the exact output generated by the following sets of statements.

    a)
```
10   PRINT TAB(10);"STUDENT";TAB(19)"STUDENT"
20   PRINT TAB(11);"NAME";TAB(20);"NUMBER"
30   LET S=5257
40   LET N$="JOHN JOHNSON"
50   PRINT TAB(10);S;TAB(17);N$
60   END
```

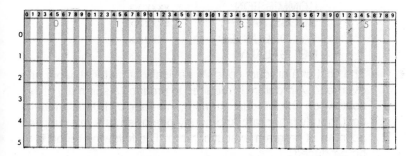

    b)
```
10   N1=3
20   N2=15
30   N3= .20
40   PRINT TAB(5);N1;
50   PRINT TAB(10);N2;
60   PRINT TAB(15);N3
70   PRINT "SUM";TAB(11);N1+N2+N3;
80   PRINT TAB(20);"PRODUCT";TAB(30);N1*N2*N3
90   END
```

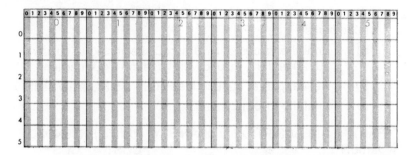

4. Rewrite the statements in Question 3 (a and b) to produce the same output, but use the PRINT USING statement instead of the TAB function.

5. A salesman receives a basic salary plus a commission of 10% on his total sales. Read the salesman's name, amount of sales, basic salary and income tax percentage. Compute the commission, income tax, gross salary and net salary. Print the following report so that the fields begin in the indicated columns.

```
Column 5                    20      26
        PAYROLL REPORT FOR   xxxxxxxxxxxxxxxxxxx
        BASIC SALARY         xxxx.xx
        COMMISSION           xxxx.xx
        GROSS SALARY         xxxx.xx
        TAX DEDUCTED          xxx.xx
        NET SALARY           xxxx.xx
```

6. The cost of a product consists basically of material, labor and overhead. A program is required to produce a summary of this cost when the product number, number of hours, material cost, hourly labor rate and hourly overhead rate are supplied as input at program execution time. The following report is to be produced.

```
                   PRODUCT COST SUMMARY

PRODUCT MATERIAL  HOURS   LABOR LABOR OVERHEAD OVER
 NUMBER   COST   WORKED   RATE  COST    RATE     CO
xxxxxxx  xxxx.xxx  xxxx   xxx.xx xxxx.xx  xxx.xx   xxx
             TOTAL PRODUCT COST xxxxx.xxx
```

6
Program
Control
Statements

When it becomes necessary to perform a set of instructions several times, there are two ways that this can be done. The first way is simply to rewrite the instructions, as in the following example, which prints the numbers from 1 to 5.

Example 1

```
00010  N=1
00020  PRINT N
00030  N=N+1
00040  PRINT N
00050  N=N+1
00060  PRINT N
00070  N=N+1
00080  PRINT N
00090  N=N+1
00100  PRINT N
00110  END
```

```
1
2
3
4
5
```

The other way is actually to reexecute the existing instructions, as shown by the following program, which uses a control statement (GO TO) at line 40.

Example 2

```
00010  N=1
00020  PRINT N
00030  N=N+1
00040  GO TO 20
00050  END
```

```
1
2
3
4
5
6
7
8
9
```

In this particular example, notice that the printed numbers do not stop at 5. In fact, this program would never stop, at least not on its own. Someone would have to intervene if the computer were ever to be used for anything besides counting.

Example 3

This example represents a simple payroll program that reads four fields: employee number (E), hours worked (H), hourly rate (R) and tax percentage (T). The program computes gross pay (G), tax (T1) and net pay (N) and prints the results of these calculations.

```
010 PRINT USING 20,
020:   NO.      HOURS      RATE        TAX          GROSS        NET
030 READ E,H,R,T
040 G=H*R
050 T1=T*G
060 N=G-T1
070 PRINT USING 80,E,H,R,T1,G,N
080:  ####     ##.#    ##.##    ####.##    ####.##    ####.##
090 DATA 3456,35.5,5.50,.15
100 END
```

```
NO.      HOURS      RATE       TAX       GROSS       NET
3456      35.5      5.50      29.29     195.25     165.96
```

The payroll program shown in Example 3 might be acceptable if there were only one employee in the company; however, in a real-world situation, it is normal for several employees to be handled in the same way. It is time consuming, monotonous and extremely inefficient to write a separate set of instructions for each employee. Therefore, it is preferable to use a control statement, the GO TO, to cause repetition of the required set of instructions for each employee.

GO TO STATEMENT

The general format of the GO TO statement is shown in Figure 6.1. The GO TO statement causes a "branch" to the statement containing the number identified by the GO TO. Transfer of control is made from the current statement to the statement number specified which will be the next statement processed by the computer. For example, the statement

95   GO TO 30

transfers control to statement number 30.

---

statement number   GO TO   statement number

FIGURE 6.1   GO TO Statement—General Format

Figure 6.2 shows that the payroll program in Example 1 can be easily changed to cause the repetition of some of the statements so that payroll information for several employees can be calculated. The message at the end, END OF DATA..., shows that no more data could be found when the READ command was issued by statement number 30. We will consider this problem further in the section on the IF statement in this chapter.

```
010 PRINT USING 20,
020:    NO.      HOURS      RATE      TAX       GROSS       NET
030 READ E,H,R,T
040 G=H*R
050 T1=T*G
060 N=G-T1
070 PRINT USING 80,E,H,R,T1,G,N
080:  ####      ##.#      ##.##    ####.##    ####.##    ####.##
085 GO TO 30
090 DATA 3456,35.5,5.50,.15
091 DATA 4567,40,4.55,.13
092 DATA 2345,24.5,5.25,.15
100 END
```

NO.	HOURS	RATE	TAX	GROSS	NET
3456	35.5	5.50	29.29	195.25	165.96
4567	40.0	4.55	23.66	182.00	158.34
2345	24.5	5.25	19.29	128.63	109.33

END OF DATA FOUND AT LINE 030 OF MAIN PROGRAM

FIGURE 6.2   Repetition of Statements

Example 4

The following program prints a request for two numbers to be

```
10 PRINT "TYPE IN 2 NUMBERS"
20 INPUT A,B
30 LET P=A*B
40 PRINT "THE PRODUCT OF";A;"AND";B;"IS";P
50 GO TO 10
60 END
```

```
TYPE IN 2 NUMBERS
? 1,5
THE PRODUCT OF 1 AND 5 IS 5
TYPE IN 2 NUMBERS
? 5,7
THE PRODUCT OF 5 AND 7 IS 35
TYPE IN 2 NUMBERS
? 15,16
THE PRODUCT OF 15 AND 16 IS 240
TYPE IN 2 NUMBERS
?
```

typed in from the keyboard. The product is then calculated, and the two numbers and the product are printed. The GO TO statement in line 50 causes the steps to be repeated, with no termination. The program would continue until interrupted by the user.

COMMON ERRORS

1.   50   GO TO 60
            60   PRINT

   It is not necessary to command that a branch be taken to the next statement. Control would go there automatically without the command. A statement of this nature is one of the marks of an inexperienced programmer.

2.   400   GO TO END
            500   READ A
            600   PRINT A
            700   END

   The GO TO statement must always identify the statement to which a branch is to be made by its number, not its keyword. *Correction:* 400   GO TO 700

3.   200   GO TO 200

   This statement is an endless loop. The program would never stop.

IF STATEMENT

The GO TO statement is an unconditional branch. The IF statement is a conditional branch instruction. The difference between the two is that a comparison is made in the IF statement, and a branch occurs only if the condition is met. The general format of the IF statement is shown in Figure 6.3; the two forms shown are equivalent.

statement number	IF condition THEN	statement number
statement number	IF condition GO TO	statement number

FIGURE 6.3   IF Statement—General Format

The condition shown in Figure 6.3 must be a logical comparison, such as the one used in the following:

50   IF A=B THEN 140

The branch to statement number 140 will be taken only if the values of A and B are the same. There are several comparison operators that may be used in BASIC; these are shown in Figure 6.4.

```
=      EQUAL TO

>      GREATER THAN

<      LESS THAN

>=     GREATER THAN OR EQUAL TO

<=     LESS THAN OR EQUAL TO

><  ⎫
    ⎬  NOT EQUAL TO
<>  ⎭
```

FIGURE 6.4

When variables are compared in the IF statement, the values are not affected. The variables may be used in subsequent statements since they retain their former values.

STRING COMPARISON

The comparison operators in Figure 6.4 may be used to compare alphanumeric data as well as numbers. The comparisons are based on the ASCII codes, which are shown in Appendix E. The coding system has been chosen in such a way that all numbers 0 to 9 are greater in value than all of the letters A to Z. By use of this collating sequence, data can be tested for sequence or arranged in alphabetical order, as shown in the following:

```
00010   LET K$ = "SMITH"
00020   LET N$ = "BROWN"
00030   IF K$=N$ THEN 60
00040   PRINT K$;" COMES BEFORE ";N$
00050   GO TO 70
00060   PRINT N$;" COMES BEFORE ";K$
00070   END
BROWN COMES BEFORE SMITH
```

THE DECISION BLOCK AND THE IF STATEMENT

The following flowcharts and BASIC statements show how the IF statement can be used.

Example 5

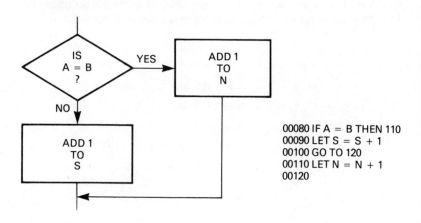

00080 IF A = B THEN 110
00090 LET S = S + 1
00100 GO TO 120
00110 LET N = N + 1
00120

Example 6

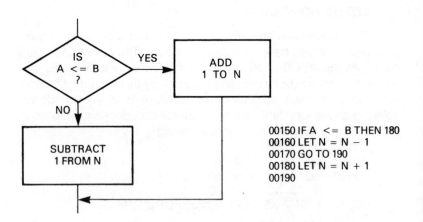

00150 IF A <= B THEN 180
00160 LET N = N − 1
00170 GO TO 190
00180 LET N = N + 1
00190

Example 7

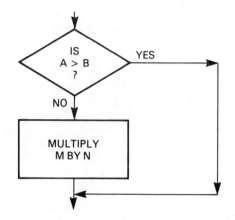

00040 IF A > B THEN 60
00050 LET M = M * N
00060

Example 8

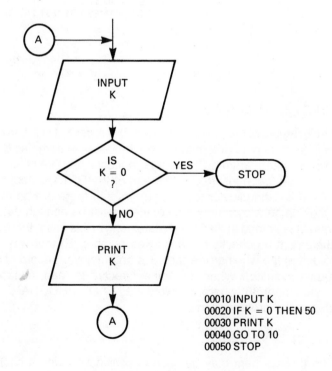

00010 INPUT K
00020 IF K = 0 THEN 50
00030 PRINT K
00040 GO TO 10
00050 STOP

Example 9

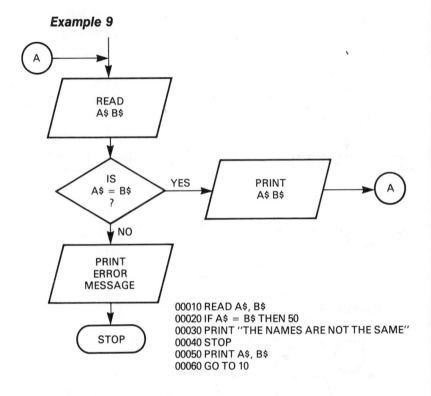

```
00010 READ A$, B$
00020 IF A$ = B$ THEN 50
00030 PRINT "THE NAMES ARE NOT THE SAME"
00040 STOP
00050 PRINT A$, B$
00060 GO TO 10
```

FINDING THE END OF DATA

The example of the payroll (Figure 6.2) is repeated in Figure 6.5 with an IF statement to determine when the last data item has been read. Notice that a "dummy" data record, containing '9999' in employee no., has been inserted at the end of the DATA statements; this is used as an indicator to the program that there are no more employees. In such a dummy record, there must be enough data to fill all variables named in the READ statement; in this case, there are four. Statement 35 checks the employee number (E) that was just read to determine whether the record is an employee record or the end-of-data indicator. When the "nines" record is read, control is sent to statement 86, where the words "END OF PROGRAM" are printed, and the program ends.

COUNTER VARIABLE

The IF statement may be used in conjunction with a counter variable to cause a sequence of instructions to be executed a certain

```
010 PRINT USING 20,
020:   NO.    HOURS      RATE      TAX        GROSS        NET
030 READ E,H,R,T
035 IF E=9999 THEN 86
040 G=H*R
050 T1=T*G
060 N=G-T1
070 PRINT USING 80,E,H,R,T1,G,N
080:  ####        ##.#    ##.##    ####.##    ####.##    ####.##
085 GO TO 30
086 PRINT "END OF PROGRAM"
090 DATA 3456,35.5,5.50,.15
091 DATA 4567,40,4.55,.13
092 DATA 2345,24.5,5.25,.15
093 DATA 9999,9,9,9
100 END
```

```
         NO.    HOURS    RATE      TAX       GROSS       NET
        3456    35.5     5.50     29.29     195.25     165.96
        4567    40.0     4.55     23.66     182.00     158.34
        2345    24.5     5.25     19.29     128.63     109.33
     END OF PROGRAM
```

FIGURE 6.5   Finding the End of Data

```
010 C=0
020 READ A,B
030 C=C+1
040 PRINT C,A,B,A*B
050 IF C<10 THEN 20
060 DATA 5,8
070 DATA 7,20
080 DATA 41,9
090 DATA 12,52
100 DATA 3,113
110 DATA 67,2
120 DATA 24,7
130 DATA 35,82
140 DATA 60,45
150 DATA 94,5
160 END
```

```
    1        5        8        40
    2        7       20       140
    3       41        9       369
    4       12       52       624
    5        3      113       339
    6       67        2       134
    7       24        7       168
    8       35       82      2870
    9       60       45      2700
   10       94        5       470
```

FIGURE 6.6   Using a Counter Variable

number of times. This is illustrated in Figure 6.6, where ten sets of data are read and printed. The counter variable (C) is incremented and checked each iteration. When C equals 10, control passes through, and the program ends.

IF STATEMENT EXAMPLES

Example 10

This program shows how the values 1 through 5 could be printed and the program could decide that it should stop, based on the value of the counter.

```
10  N=1
20  PRINT N
30  N=N+1
40  IF N ≤ 6 THEN 20
50  END
```

```
1
2
3
4
5
```

Example 11

A company has the policy of offering a discount to customers who buy in large quantities. If the amount of an invoice is over $500.00, a discount is allowed. The company would like to know what percentage of the orders qualified for a discount last week. Write a program to calculate and print the percentage. The DATA records contain an invoice number (I) and a sale amount (A). The last DATA statement is recognized by an invoice number 9999.

```
00010 READ I,A
00020 IF I=9999 THEN 70
00030 T=T+1
00040 IF A<=500 THEN 10
00050 D=D+1
00060 GO TO 10
00070 P=D/T*100
00080 PRINT P;"%OF INVOICES QUALIFY"
00090 DATA 1246,499.99
00100 DATA 2910,500.01
00110 DATA 8261,250.30
00120 DATA 2346,1000.25
00130 DATA 8828,450.98
00140 DATA 6193,2671.85
00150 DATA 9200,5.01
00160 DATA 1626,147.88
00170 DATA 7262,749.02
00180 DATA 3265,612.50
00190 DATA 5118,962.83
00200 DATA 2608,999.99
00210 DATA 9999,9
00220 END

  58.33333 %OF INVOICES QUALIFY
```

In the program, the total number of records is maintained in T, and the number qualifying for discount in D. The percentage (P) is calculated at the end and is then printed.

Example 12

The following program shows a sales commission program that illustrates some of the principles of the use of the GO TO and IF statements. The DATA records contain salesman's number (S), name (N$) and the amount sold (A). The salesman's commission is calculated based on the amount sold, as shown in the following table.

Amount Sold	Commission
less than $1000.00	5%
$1000.00—$1999.99	7%
$2000.00—$2999.99	10%
$3000.00 or more	12%

Since there may be a large number of DATA records, the heading is repeated after 10 lines of output. This is accomplished by using a line counter (L), which is incremented each time a line is printed (statement 420). The frequency of the heading repetition is easily changed, by modifying statement 430 to test for any particular value.

Two image statements are used: one causes a dollar sign to be inserted and is used only after the heading; the other, without the dollar sign, is used for all the rest.

```
010 LET L=0
020 PRINT
030 PRINT
040 PRINT "SALES NO.","NAME","AMOUNT","COMMISSION"
050 PRINT
060 READ S,N$,A
070 IF S=999 THEN 450
080 IF A<1000 THEN 200
090 IF A<2000 THEN 300
100 IF A<3000 THEN 400
110 C=A*.12
120 GO TO 401
200 LET C=A*.05
210 GO TO 401
300 LET C=A*.07
310 GO TO 401
400 LET C=A*.10
401 IF L>0 THEN 410
402 PRINT USING 403,S,N$,A,C
403:    ###       'LLLLLLLLLL   $####.##            $####.##
404 GO TO 420
410 PRINT USING 415,S,N$,A,C
415:    ###       'LLLLLLLLLL   ####.##             ####.##
420 L=L+1
430 IF L=10 THEN 10
440 GO TO 60
```

```
450 PRINT "END OF PROGRAM"
460 DATA 100,J ABEL,500
461 DATA 115,S BELL,115
462 DATA 119,A CAVE,1500
463 DATA 225,C CHART,3100
464 DATA 226,Q CRUZ,100
465 DATA 278,D DE LANE,2000
466 DATA 305,F FLIN,3000
467 DATA 330,J FULTON,5000
468 DATA 365,A GRAY,2300
469 DATA 400,L HOBBS,1990
470 DATA 444,W LAKELAND,3300
471 DATA 470,N PARKER,1999
472 DATA 500,R MOORE,4000
473 DATA 554,F PRATT,3900
474 DATA 599,V SMITH,1400
475 DATA 999,LAST,0
500 END
```

SALES NO.	NAME	AMOUNT	COMMISSION
100	J ABEL	$ 500.00	$ 25.00
115	S BELL	115.00	5.75
119	A CAVE	1500.00	105.00
225	C CHART	3100.00	372.00
226	Q CRUZ	100.00	5.00
278	D DE LANE	2000.00	200.00
305	F FLIN	3000.00	360.00
330	J FULTON	5000.00	600.00
365	A GRAY	2300.00	230.00
400	L HOBBS	1990.00	139.30

SALES NO.	NAME	AMOUNT	COMMISSION
444	W LAKELAND	$3300.00	$ 396.00
470	N PARKER	1999.00	139.93
500	R MOORE	4000.00	480.00
554	F PRATT	3900.00	468.00
598	V SMITH	1400.00	98.00

END OF PROGRAM

COMMON ERRORS

1.   50   IF A = B THEN STOP

This is usually incorrect because no action may be specified as a result of a comparison. (However, some BASIC systems do allow this.) The IF statement is a conditional branch, meaning that the only acceptable entry after the word THEN is a statement number. *Correction:*   50   IF A = B THEN 200

—
—
—

200   STOP

2.   80   IF A > B THEN GO TO 30

Here too, BASIC would find the words GO TO instead of simply the statement number.
Correction: 80 IF A > B THEN 30 or
80 IF A > B GO TO 30

3.   150   IF A$ = YES THEN 45

If an alphanumeric value is to be compared with a literal, the literal must be enclosed by quotation marks.
Correction: 150   IF A$ = "YES" THEN 45

4.   100   IF A=> B THEN 500

In most BASIC systems, only the comparison operators shown in Figure 6.4 are valid. These symbols are reversed.
Correction: 100   IF A > =B THEN 500

5.   125   IF A< B OR A<C THEN 70

Multiple comparisons are not allowed in most BASIC systems. If more than one comparison must be made, there must be an IF statement for each test. Words such as OR, AND, NOT and IS may not be used.
Correction: 125   IF A< B THEN 70
126   IF A<C THEN 70
130

This set of commands tests to see whether either condition is true and then branches. It is possible to test for both conditions before branching, as follows:

125   IF A< B THEN 127
126   GO TO 130
127   IF A<C THEN 70
130

ON—GO TO STATEMENT

In some programs, a variable may have a range of consecutive values. For instance, a variable may represent a code indicating marital status as follows:

Code	Meaning
1	Single
2	Married
3	Separated
4	Divorced
5	Widowed

The conventional approach to using these codes is to use a sequence of IF statements to transfer control to the proper statement for each code.

```
90    READ N$,M
100   IF M = 1 THEN 150
110   IF M = 2 THEN 250
120   IF M = 3 THEN 310
130   IF M = 4 THEN 380
140   IF M = 5 THEN 440
```

In this illustration, M represents the marital status code, and N$ is the name. Depending on the value of M, the program will branch to the statement number required (150 if M equals 1, 250 if M is 2, etc.). In this situation, an ON—GO TO statement could be used; its general format is shown in Figure 6.7.

---

statement number ON   variable expression   GO TO sn1, sn2, sn3,...

sn1, sn2, etc. are statement numbers to which control will be sent based on the value of the variable or the evaluation of the expression.

FIGURE 6.7   ON—GO TO—General Format

USING A VARIABLE

The marital status program could be rewritten with an ON—GO TO statement since the variable M has a range of consecutive values from 1 to 5. The statements might look like this:

```
90    READ N$,M
100   ON M GO TO 150,250,310,380,440
```

Just as before, if M equals 1, control is passed to statement 150; if M is 2, control is transferred to statement 250; etc. If the value of M is not within the proper range, an error occurs.

USING AN EXPRESSION

Suppose that the code for marital status were not assigned as conveniently, such as if 10, 11, 12, 13 and 14 were the indicators. The ON—GO TO statement could still be used and be written as:

$$100 \quad ON \ M\text{-}9 \ GO \ TO \ 150,250,310,380,440$$

When M-9 is calculated, the result is a value within the range of 1—5, which satisfies the requirements of the ON—GO TO.

If the codes were 10, 20, 30, 40 and 50, the statement would be:

$$100 \quad ON \ M/10 \ GO \ TO \ 150,250,310,380,440$$

When M is divided by 10, the result is again within the range of 1—5, which would be used to cause a branch to the proper routine.

COMMON ERRORS

1. 40 K = 5
    50 ON K GO TO 100,200,300

    The value of K could be 1, 2 or 3 and still be valid. Any value larger than 3 results in an error since there are only three statement numbers in the ON—GO TO statement.

2. 100   ON A$ GO TO 50,150,250

    The variable must be numeric.
    Correction: 100   ON A GO TO 50,150,250

FOR—NEXT STATEMENTS

By using the IF statement and/or the GO TO statement, we have been able to cause the instructions of a program to be executed many times. This process is called looping, and each pass through the instructions is one iteration. The FOR—NEXT statements allow an easy method of causing a set of instructions to be executed a certain number of times. The general format of these instructions is shown in Figure 6.8.

---

statement number   FOR variable = value-1 TO value-2 STEP value-3
                    —
                    —
statement number   NEXT variable

FIGURE 6.8   FOR—NEXT Statements—General Format

In Figure 6.8, value-1, value-2 and value-3 may be numbers, variables, expressions or a combination of these. They may not be alphanumeric values. Their meanings are as follows:

value-1: the initial or starting value

value-2: the terminal or final value

value-3: the increment value, which may be omitted if the variable is increased by 1 each iteration

Example 13: Advantages of Using For—Next Statements

Both of the following programs read and print 10 times. The first program uses a counter variable and GO TO and IF statements. The values A and B are read from the data and subsequently printed. N is printed to indicate the number of lines printed.

```
010 LET N=0
020 LET N=N+1
030 IF N>10 THEN 70
040 READ A,B
050 PRINT N,A,B
060 GO TO 20
070 PRINT "END OF PROGRAM"
080 DATA 5,88
090 DATA 32,9
100 DATA 7,3
110 DATA 4,9
120 DATA 50,3
130 DATA 54,8
140 DATA 24,6
150 DATA 16,7
160 DATA 81,9
170 DATA 95,5
180 END
```

```
1          5          88
2          32         9
3          7          3
4          4          9
5          50         3
6          54         8
7          24         6
8          16         7
9          81         9
10         95         5
END OF PROGRAM
```

The second program uses the FOR—NEXT statements to control the looping of the program through the 10 iterations. The value of N is printed to show its changing value as the DATA statements are read and printed. Notice that N starts at 1 (initial value), increases by 1 for each iteration (increment value) and stops at 10 (terminal value).

With the initial, terminal and increment values being specified, BASIC takes over the control of the loop, leaving us simply to state what should be done for each iteration.

```
010 FOR N=1 TO 10 STEP 1
020 READ A,B
030 PRINT N,A,B
040 NEXT N
050 PRINT "END OF PROGRAM"
060 DATA 5,88
070 DATA 32,9
080 DATA 7,3
090 DATA 4,9
100 DATA 50,3
110 DATA 54,8
120 DATA 24,6
130 DATA 16,7
140 DATA 81,9
150 DATA 95,5
160 END
```

```
1               5               88
2               32              9
3               7               3
4               4               9
5               50              3
6               54              8
7               24              6
8               16              7
9               81              9
10              95              5
END OF PROGRAM
```

Example 14

Two programs are shown in this example. The first shows a counter and an IF statement controlling the loop; the second uses FOR—NEXT statements. The results are identical.

```
10 N=1
20 PRINT N;
30 N=N+1
40 IF N<6 THEN 20
50 END
```

```
1  2  3  4  5
```

```
10 FOR N=1 TO 5 STEP 1
20 PRINT N;
30 NEXT N
40 END
```

```
1  2  3  4  5
```

Example 15:   *Summing A Series of Numbers*

In this example, we are going to find the sum of all the integers from 1 to 100 (1+2+3+...+97+98+99+100). Again, the first program does not use FOR—NEXT statements to control the loop, the second does.

```
10 LET S=0
20 LET C=0
30 LET C=C+1
40 IF C>100 THEN 70
50 LET S=S+C
60 GO TO 30
70 PRINT "THE SUM OF 1 TO 100 IS";S
80 END
THE SUM OF 1 TO 100 IS 5050

10 LET S=0
20 FOR C=1 TO 100
30 LET S=S+C
40 NEXT C
50 PRINT "THE SUM OF 1 TO 100 IS";S
60 END
THE SUM OF 1 TO 100 IS 5050
```

This program could be modified easily to calculate the sum of the set of numbers from 1 to any desired value. The program with such modifications is shown here. The terminal number must be typed in by the user in response to the request by the program. This too could be made more general by allowing the user to specify both the initial and terminal values. By including a PRINT statement inside the FOR—NEXT loop, a running total can be shown.

```
10 INPUT "TYPE IN THE TERMINAL NUMBER",T
20 FOR C=1 TO T
30 LET S=S+C
40 NEXT C
50 PRINT "THE SUM OF 1 TO";T;"IS";S
60 END

TYPE IN THE TERMINAL NUMBER  ? 25
THE SUM OF 1 TO 25 IS 325

10 LET S=0
20 INPUT "TYPE IN THE INITIAL AND TERMINAL NUMBERS",I,T
30 FOR C=I TO T
40 LET S=S+C
50 NEXT C
60 PRINT "THE SUM OF";I;"TO";T;"IS";S
70 END

TYPE IN THE INITIAL AND TERMINAL NUMBERS  ? 10,15
THE SUM OF 10 TO 15 IS 75

10 LET S=0
20 INPUT "TYPE IN THE INITIAL AND TERMINAL NUMBERS",I,T
30 FOR C=I TO T
40 LET S=S+C
50 PRINT S
60 NEXT C
70 PRINT "THE SUM OF";I;"TO";T;"IS";S
80 END

TYPE IN THE INITIAL AND TERMINAL NUMBERS  ? 10,15
 10
 21
 33
 46
 60
 75
THE SUM OF 10 TO 15 IS 75
```

NESTED LOOPS

More than one FOR—NEXT loop may be used in a program to cause one FOR—NEXT loop to be controlled by another. This is called nesting and is demonstrated by the following program.

```
10 PRINT " I"," J"
20 PRINT
30 FOR I=1 TO 4
40 FOR J=1 TO 3
50 PRINT I,J
60 NEXT J
70 NEXT I
80 END
```

I	J
1	1
1	2
1	3
2	1
2	2
2	3
3	1
3	2
3	3
4	1
4	2
4	3

When this program is executed, the characters I and J are printed as a heading. The value of I is set at 1, and the first loop is started. The value of J is then set at 1, and the inner loop is entered. The PRINT statement is executed (there may be many statements or very few statements inside a loop), showing the first values of I and J. Statement 60 causes J to be incremented by 1, giving J the value of 2. The inner loop is then repeated, printing the values of I (1) and J (2). Once again J is increased by 1, to the value 3, and the loop is reexecuted, printing the values 1 and 3. At this point, J has reached its terminal value, and control passes to statement 70, where I becomes 2. The outer loop is again executed; since the inner loop is part of it, J is set at 1, and the sequence is repeated. The output of the whole program is shown by the listing.

Example 16:   Sum of the Cube of the Digits

Find all the positive 3-digit numbers (100-999) whose value is equal to the sum of the cube of the digits. To get around the words, look at the following example:

$$153 = 1^3 + 5^3 + 3^3$$

This program has three nested FOR—NEXT loops. The inner loop controls N1, which represents the units position of the numbers; N2 is the tens position and is controlled by the middle loop; and N3 is controlled by the outer loop, and represents the hundreds position.

```
010 FOR N3=1 TO 9
020 FOR N2=0 TO 9
030 FOR N1=0 TO 9
040 A=(N1↑3)+(N2↑3)+(N3↑3)
050 B=N1+(N2*10)+(N3*100)
060 IF A=B THEN 80
070 GO TO 90
080 PRINT B
090 NEXT N1
100 NEXT N2
110 NEXT N3
130 END

153
370
371
407
```

Example 17:   Change for a Dollar

Find how many ways it is possible to make change for $1.00. (This one may take your computer some time to calculate).
The variables in this program have the following meaning:

Variable	Represents
F	Half Dollar
Q	Quarter
D	Dime
N	Nickel
P	Penny
C	Counter

Statement 60 tests the value represented by the sum of the various coins. At first, F is 0 (zero), meaning that there are no half dollars represented; Q is 0, meaning that there are no quarters; etc. The value of P goes from 0 up to 99 without finding a combination that adds up to 100. This occurs because the value of P is controlled by the innermost loop and therefore increases through its range without affecting the values of any of the other variables.

The first combination to add up to 100 is 100 pennies. When this occurs, C (the counter) is increased by 1. C is increased once more when there are 95 pennies and 1 nickel. This process is repeated with all possible coin combinations, and, when the value of a given combination adds up to 100, C is increased. The final value of the counter is printed at the end.

```
010 FOR F=0 TO 2
020 FOR Q=0 TO 4
030 FOR D=0 TO 10
040 FOR N=0 TO 20
050 FOR P=0 TO 100
060 IF (F*50)+(Q*25)+(D*10)+(N*5)+P = 100 THEN 80
070 GO TO 90
080 C=C+1
090 NEXT P
100 NEXT N
110 NEXT D
120 NEXT Q
130 NEXT F
140 PRINT "THERE ARE";C;"WAYS TO CHANGE $1.00"
150 END

THERE ARE 292 WAYS TO CHANGE $1.00
```

COMMON ERRORS

1. `10  FOR A$=1 TO 50`

    Only numeric values may be used. *Correction:* 10   FOR A=1 TO 50

2.  ```
    50  FOR N=1 TO 10
    60  LET T=T+N
    70  PRINT T
    80  END
    ```

    There is no NEXT statement. The correction would be to place the NEXT statement at the appropriate point.

3.  ```
    600  FOR C=1 TO 100
    700  C=2
    800  NEXT C
    ```

    The value of C would never reach 100. It is set at 2 in statement number 700 for every iteration. This is a logic error, the correction of which depends on the desired result. It is rarely correct to alter the value of the FOR variable inside the loop.

4.  ```
    100  FOR I=1 TO 10
    110  READ V
    120  GO TO 100
    130  NEXT I
    ```

    This would result in an endless loop since I is not incremented by the NEXT at statement number 130. The value of I would be set at 1 every time control is sent to statement 100. *Correction:* Remove statement 120.
    ```

5. 10 FOR K=1 TO 5
    20 READ N
    30 IF N > 10 THEN 50
    40 NEXT K
    50 LET C=C+1
    60 NEXT K

    There must be only one NEXT statement at the end of the
    loop. *Correction:* 40   GO TO 60

6. 50 FOR A=5 TO 1
    60 LET D=D-A
    70 NEXT A

    The initial value must not be greater than the terminal value
    unless a negative step value is supplied.
    Correction: 50   FOR A=5 TO 1 STEP −1

7. 10 FOR I=1 TO 10
    20 FOR K=1 TO 5
    30 LET N=I*K
    40 PRINT N
    50 NEXT I
    60 NEXT K

    The FOR—NEXT loops are not properly nested. The inner
    loop must be completely contained within the outer loop.
    Correction: 10   FOR I=1 TO 10
    20 FOR K=1 TO 5
    30 LET N=I*K
    40 PRINT N
    50 NEXT K
    60 NEXT I

QUESTIONS

1. Identify the errors in each of the following statements.

    a) 50   IF X < Y THEN GO TO 10
    b) 100 FOR N=1 TO C$
    c) 30   GO TO PRINT
            40   LET N=5
            50   LET T=4
            60   PRINT A,B
    d) 60   FOR I=1 TO 10
            70   PRINT I,I↑2
            80   END
    e) 100 ON N$ GO TO 150,275,340
    f) 10   FOR A=1 TO 5 STEP 1
            20   LET T=T+A
            30   GO TO 10
            40   NEXT A
    g) 50   N=3
            60   N=N+3
            70   ON N GO TO 200,500,700
    h) 240 IF X = 1 OR 5 THEN 60
    i) 745 IF I = 10 THEN STOP
    j) 175 IF K =>5 THEN 200
            190 GO TO 55
            200 PRINT K

2. Write statements to do the following.

    a) Use a FOR—NEXT loop to print the odd numbers from 1 to 50.

    b) Use a FOR—NEXT loop to sum the integers from 25 to 50.

    c) Use a FOR—NEXT loop to sum the integers from 15 to 30. Print a running total.

    d) Use a FOR—NEXT loop to control the reading and printing of ten data records, each containing a name (N$) and an amount (A). Print the total of the amounts at the end.

    e) Five salesmen are numbered consecutively from 101 to 105. Write a program to read data records with a salesman's number and an amount, and use an ON—GO TO statement to accumulate the total sales for each salesman. The last data record has a salesman's number 999.

3. What would be printed (exactly, on each line) by each of the following programs?

a)
```
10  READ N
20  LET C=5
30  LET D=3
40  LET B=D+C
50  IF B > N THEN 80
60  PRINT "B IS SMALL"
70  STOP
80  PRINT "B IS LARGE"
90  DATA 7
100 END
```

b)
```
10  A=6
20  B=2
30  READ N
40  LET C=A*B
50  IF C>= N THEN 90
60  PRINT A,B,"FINAL"
70  STOP
80  LET B=B+1
90  PRINT "NOT YET"
100 GO TO 40
110 DATA 24
120 END
```

c)
```
10  PRINT "HELLO"
20  LET T=7
30  LET M=3
40  LET R=T-M
50  IF R=0 THEN 90
60  PRINT "HELLO AGAIN"
70  LET M=M+1
80  GO TO 40
90  PRINT "GOODBYE"
100 END
```

d)
```
10  READ A,B,C
20  IF A=B-C THEN 70
30  IF A=B*C THEN 90
40  IF A=B+C THEN 110
50  PRINT "NO MATCH"
60  STOP
```

```
         70    PRINT "DIFFERENCE"
         80    STOP
         90    PRINT "PRODUCT"
        100    STOP
        110    PRINT "SUM"
        120    DATA 4,2,2
        130    END
 e)      10    B=0
         20    READ A
         30    IF A=9999 THEN 90
         40    IF A < B THEN 70
         50    B=A
         60    GO TO 20
         70    PRINT "THE NUMBERS ARE NOT IN SEQUENCE"
         80    STOP
         90    PRINT "THE NUMBERS ARE IN SEQUENCE"
        100    DATA 1037
        110    DATA 1597
        120    DATA 1598
        130    DATA 1724
        140    DATA 1811
        150    DATA 1926
        160    DATA 1985
        170    DATA 9999
        180    END
 f)      10    READ A,B,C
         20    IF A=99 THEN 220
         30    ON A GO TO 40,70,100
         40    D=D*C
         50    PRINT "PRODUCT IS ";D
         60    GO TO 10
         70    D=B+C
         80    PRINT "SUM IS ";D
         90    GO TO 10
        100    IF B > C THEN 130
        110    D=C-B
        120    GO TO 140
        130    D=B-C
        140    PRINT "DIFFERENCE IS ";D
        150    GO TO 10
        160    DATA 2,12,91
        170    DATA 3,140,32
```

```
180   DATA 1,8,25
190   DATA 3,65,80
200   DATA 1,15,16
210   DATA 99,9,9
220   END
```

4. Consider the following series:
                   1, 2, 4, 7, 11, 16,...
    Write a program to generate and print the first 25 numbers in
    the series.

5. Read two numbers from a data card. Depending on which
    number is larger, print either FIRST or SECOND.

6. Write a program that produces the following table, including
    headings, for the numbers 1 to 35 inclusive.

N	SUM OF N	N SQUARED	SUM OF N SQUARED
1	1	1	1
2	3	4	5
3	6	9	14
.			
.			
.			
35			

7. Data cards contain student number and the number of days
    that the student has been absent. Print the student number
    and the days absent for any student absent 9 or more days.

8. Manhattan Island was purchased from the Indians in 1626 for
    $24.00. If the Indians had invested the money at 6% interest
    compounded annually, what would be the value of the invest-
    ment at the end of the following years: 1680, 1780, 1880 and
    1980?

9. The population of Waterloo in 1975 was 50,000. The popula-
    tion of Toronto in that year was 2,200,000. Waterloo grows at
    10% per year while Toronto grows at 2%. Assuming a con-
    stant growth rate, in what year will the population of Waterloo
    be as large as that of Toronto? Print the final population fig-
    ures.

10. A salesman has made many sales. He wants to know how
    many were $100.00 or less, how many between $100.00 and
    $200.00 and how many were over $200.00. Data cards con-
    tain an invoice number and the sale amount. Use 15—20 data
    cards.

11.   Cards contain part number, quantity and cost. Print a report showing part number, quantity, cost and extended cost. At the end of the report, print the total extended cost. Use 10 data cards or more.

12.   An apartment house has 200 units. With a monthly rental of $175 per unit, all apartments are rented. For each $2.00 increase in monthly rental, one apartment will become vacant; for example, rent is $177, 199 units will be rented. The owner of the building wishes to maximize his income and therefore will increase the rent to the point where total rent is at a maximum. Write a program to determine the rent per unit that will bring maximum revenue. Print the monthly rent, number of units occupied and the total monthly revenue. Use no data cards.

13.   A class of students is represented by a deck of cards, each card containing student number, age and average grade. Print the data for all students 19 or older who have an average of 95% or higher. At the end of the report, show the total number of students, the number of students printed and the percentage of students printed. Use 15—25 data cards.

14.   Print a class list from cards containing student number, number of subjects and average grade. At the end, print the number of students and the class average. Use 15 or more data cards.

15.   Prepare a report listing charitable donations by employees. Accumulate the total donation, calculate the average donation, and print these at the end of the report.
There should be only one card per employee. The cards contain employee number and donation amount. If more than one card is found for an employee, the program must print a message and stop. The cards are in sequence by employee number. If a card is found to be out of sequence, the program must again print a message and stop.
Use 10 or more data cards, and be sure that the program will handle cards out of sequence, and duplicate cards.

16.   A computer dating service wishes to produce a report of all single females between 19 and 21, inclusive, who have blue eyes and blond hair. Examine the codes in the data records to produce this report.

Data Record	Fields	Codes
Name		
Address		
Phone	Number	
Age		
Sex		1 — Male
		2 — Female
Marital Status		1 — Single
		2 — Married
		3 — Divorced
		4 — Separated
Eye Color		1 — Brown
		2 — Green
		3 — Blue
Hair Color		1 — Blond
		2 — Brunette
		3 — Red

17. Using the data records for question 16, determine the number of males and females in each marital status. Print these eight totals and indicate the percentage each of them represent of the entire data.

18. Write a program to find all the prime numbers between 1 and 100.

19. A student plans to save $40.00 per month leaving school at 21 until he retires at age 65. Given an annual interest rate of 8% computed and compounded quarterly, what will his investment be worth on his retirement?

20. A company requires a payroll report that lists the earnings for each employee in each department. Totals are required at the end of each department, and overall totals are required at the end of the report. Each record must be in sequence by employee number within department number, and the program must be terminated if a sequence error occurs. The number of departments and the number of employees per department are unknown. The data records, one per employee, contain:

Department Number	3 digits
Employee Number	5 digits
Hours Worked	3 digits
Hourly Rate	4 digits (2 decimal)
Tax Percentage	2 digits (both decimal)
Deductions	5 digits (2 decimal)

7
Program Debugging and Testing

One of the most important tasks facing a new programmer is learning to debug a program successfully. Few people are able to write a program and to have it run correctly the first time. In fact it is not unusual to spend as much time testing and debugging a program as writing the program initially.

To debug successfully requires the development of new skills to supplement the programming skills of the individual. By following certain predefined steps, a program may be debugged and made to work in the way that the programmer originally intended.

The major debugging and testing considerations that we will discuss are:

1. Desk Checking

2. Syntax and Semantic Errors

3. Test Data Preparation

4. Tracing Program Logic

Generally, testing proceeds in this order, but changes to the program at any time can cause the programmer to go back to any of the earlier steps. This may be the result of errors that were overlooked previously or because of new errors that were introduced during the testing process.

DESK CHECKING

This is probably the easiest of all debugging techniques and yet the most often overlooked. After careful planning and flowcharting of the solution, the programmer will write the BASIC code. Coding the program should be done on paper, not at the terminal or keypunch. Use of block lettering, not writing, will reduce errors made when the program is keypunched or keyed into a data entry device. At this point, take some time to desk check the code. If the program was keypunched, examine the cards (hopefully they were interpreted); if a terminal was used, read the printout. It is surprising how many errors can be detected at this stage without the computer's assistance. Types of errors to look for at this stage are spelling errors, keying errors, missing or duplicate statements, and statements out of order.

SYNTAX AND SEMANTIC ERRORS

This step is concerned with using the language correctly, as it is defined for a specific machine. Since each BASIC interpreter is unique in some ways, we will not attempt to discuss all types of errors but rather to provide some guidance for their correction.

Syntax refers to improper punctuation of statements in the language whereas semantics refers to the proper understanding of the statement format. This is generally discussed throughout the book, so a detailed presentation will not be given here.

Essentially, following the statement format will lead to correct semantics in your program. For example, the statement:

$$\text{FOR I FROM 1 TO N STEP K}$$

may sound OK, but it is semantically incorrect because the format of a FOR statement does not include the word FROM. Rather the = symbol must be used. Therefore the statement:

$$\text{FOR I} = \text{1 TO N STEP K}$$

is correct.

Syntax errors are many and varied. In a number of cases, it is difficult to determine whether an error is in the syntax or the semantics of a language. Although there are precise definitions of these, we are more concerned with finding the errors. The following is a list of errors that are encountered quite frequently by programmers. Most of these errors are identified by error messages from the interpreter. A list of these messages may be found in Appendix B.

Type of Error	Example	Explanation
Missing Commas	10 N(I K) = A+B	The comma separating subscripts 1 and K is missing.
	10 INPUT A B	Two variables in input and output statements must be separated by commas. Some interpreters treat this as variable AB rather than as an error.
Parentheses	10 N = N + 1) * 5 20 A=(K+1*5+(J/N)))	Either too few brackets as in statement 10 or too many as in 20 can be the cause of this problem. Make sure that all brackets are matching pairs.

Operator	10 N+N=K 20 J=B(N+L) 30 K=P*/J	In line 10, the statement is reversed; this is a common problem with new programmers. Statement 20 has the multiply operator missing after the B; some systems call this an error while others consider B to be an array and (N+L) the subscript. Statement 30 has two operators together; a variable is probably missing.
Mismatch	10A$=10 20 N="DON CASSEL"	This occurs when a numeric value is assigned to an alphanumeric variable or vice versa.
Illegal Verb	10 S=SQRT(256)	This happens when a keyword is misspelled. SQRT is valid in some languages but not in BASIC.
Arguments Do Not Match	10 DEF FNA(K,J)=K↑2+J↑3 50 PRINT FNA(16)	This error occurs when two or more arguments are possible in a function. In this case, function A uses two arguments, but the call in statement 50 supplies only one.

During program execution, errors, which are not indicated earlier, may be found. These are generally self-explanatory errors, such as dividing by zero, trying to calculate the square root of a negative number, and having arithmetic overflows or subscripts out of range.

For example, in the following case in which a constant is being used:

$$10 \text{ DIM N}(15)$$
$$50 \text{ N}(21) = T*K$$

it is evident that the subscript of 21 in statement 50 is the culprit; maybe it should have been 12, or possibly N should have been dimensioned with more elements. However, if the statement in error had been:

$$50 \text{N(I)} = T*K$$

then it would be necessary to trace the values of I to see why it had exceeded the permissible range of the subscript.

TEST DATA PREPARATION

The first rule of data preparation is that quality and not quantity is what counts. Beginning programmers often prepare a lot of data that looks impressive but which is really quite meaningless. Each item of data should have a specific purpose and therefore be testing for a specific potential problem. Some of the things for which data should be prepared to test are:

1. Sequence error

2. Missing data

3. Positive and negative values

4. Valid and invalid codes

5. Numbers within a specific range including the first and last numbers of the range

6. Too much or too little data when using tables

7. Reasonableness. An hourly rate over $100.00 is likely unreasonable.

8. Length. Fields such as phone numbers, account numbers and social insurance numbers are of predefined lengths and can be checked.

Not every program will need to test for all of these items, and some programs will need to test for other factors. The key is to be aware of possible sources of error and to consider them in your testing.

A final consideration is that test data should be supplied to check every statement of code written in the program. Do not assume that a code will work just because it is obvious or simple. Errors do not happen solely in complex codes: they often occur in the most unlikely places.

TRACING PROGRAM LOGIC

Tracing is the process of following the program logic step by step to locate an error. This can be done manually for relatively easy problems, or program statements can be used to show the flow of the logic. The key is to know what to expect from your program. If you know what output the program is intended to produce, then when it does not produce this output, a trace can be used to determine why.

MANUAL TRACING

This is done with a copy of the program listing, its output (if any) and a pencil. This method is particularly useful for small programs, simple bugs or when there is no output to check.

To show how this works, let us write a program to print a chart of Celsius and Fahrenheit temperatures. The chart is to include Celsius temperatures from 10 to 34 and their equivalent Fahrenheit temperatures as integer values. We expect the output to appear as follows:

C	F	C	F	C	F	C	F	C	F
10	50	11	51	12	53	13	55	14	57
15	59	16	60	17	62	18	64	19	66
20	68	21	69	22	71	23	73	24	75
25	77	26	78	27	80	28	82	29	84
30	86	31	87	32	89	33	91	34	93

The program written to solve this problem is as follows:

```
5    PRINT "      ";
10   FOR I = 1 TO 5
20   PRINT "C       F      ";
30   NEXT I
40   PRINT·
50   FOR I = 10 TO 30 STEP 5
60   FOR C = I TO 4
70   F = INT((C * 9) / 5 + 32)
80   PRINT C;F;
90   NEXT C
100  PRINT
110  NEXT I
120  END
```

When this program is run, the output produced is:

C	F	C	F	C	F	C	F	C	F
10	50								
15	59								
20	68								
25	77								
30	86								

Two problems are evident from this printout: first we are getting only one column of Celsius and Fahrenheit temperatures; second there are no spaces between the lines of output as indicated in the expected results.

The second problem may be easier to solve at this point. Statement 100 is used to start a new line after a full line of output, but it does not create a blank line. This can be achieved by using a second print statement at line 105 in the program.

To locate the problem of missing output, we will perform a manual trace of the program. To do this, we list the names of the variables that are used in this part of the logic. Since the heading looks OK, we do not need to trace this part of the program. The variables that might cause the problem are I, C and F. We will trace statements 50 through 110. These variables are written down as follows with an additional column that counts the number of iterations through the logic. The first time through the program code, the manual trace looks like this:

Iterations	I	C	F
1	10	10	50

Each time that we follow the code visually, we write down on the trace the effect that the code had on each variable. We are careful to do what the program says, not what we think it says. As we continue, the trace will look like this:

Iterations	I	C	F
1	10	10	50
2	15	15	59
3	20	20	68
4	25	25	77
5	30	30	86

At this point the program ends. It is not absolutely essential to continue the trace to the bitter end but only long enough to determine what is causing the error in the logic. By reading this trace, it is evident that C is not taking on all of the expected values. Since C is used to represent Celsius, it should take on each Celsius value. However, it only takes the same values as I. If we check the statement that gives C its value, we might find the error. This is statement 60, which reads:

60   FOR C=I TO 4

From this statement, it is clear that the terminating value 4 is incorrect. It should have been I+4, which would generate five values of C for each line. By changing the program to read:

                60   FOR C=I TO I+4

we get the correct output.

C	F	C	F	C	F	C	F	C	F
10	50	11	51	12	53	13	55	14	57
15	59	16	60	17	62	18	64	19	66
20	68	21	69	22	71	23	73	24	75
25	77	26	78	27	80	28	82	29	84
30	86	31	87	32	89	33	91	34	93

AUTOMATIC PROGRAM TRACING

Many programs are either too large or too complex for manual tracing except in the most limited circumstances. In such a case, it is helpful if the program can be used to perform its own tracing. This can be accomplished by placing PRINT statements at temporary locations within the program.

One use of this method is to determine whether the program reaches a specific location. This can be done by placing a print statement such as

                200 PRINT "TAX ROUTINE"

at the beginning of the program code to be tested. If the literal TAX ROUTINE prints out, we know that the program does reach this point. It is important to use a message that will not be confused with normal program output. When we are certain that the program is executing correctly or that the error has been found, statment 200 will be removed since it has served its purpose.

Another use for this type of statement is to determine the contents of variables as the program is executing. This is similar to manual tracing except that it is printed by the program. A statement might be:

                3500 PRINT I,N1

Each time that the program reaches line 3500, the contents of I and N1 are printed. The programmer then examines these values to see if they are what is expected. If not, this gives some indication of the source of the program error.

It is important to realize that this temporary trace output is printed with other output. With a little experience, it is not too difficult to separate visually the normal output from the trace. If this becomes too much of a problem, some programmers temporarily remove the other print statements so that the trace is easier to follow.

Often, the above trace methods are combined. For instance:

4350 PRINT "ORDER QUANTITY";Q;Q$

prints both a message and the contents of the variables Q and Q$ when this part of the program is reached. To demonstrate this technique of debugging, we will take another look at the Sales Commission Program. Figure 7.1 shows how the program and data might appear after the initial syntax errors have been corrected. Following the program is the output that was printed.

```
100 REM SALES COMMISSION PROGRAM
200 PRINT
300 PRINT"SALES NO.","NAME","AMOUNT","COMMISSION"
400 PRINT
500 READ S,N$,A
600 IF S=999 THEN 2100
700 IF A<1000 THEN 1300
800 IF A<2000 THEN 1400
900 IF A<3000 THEN 1600
1000 LET C=A*.12
1100 GOTO 1700
1200 LET C=A*.05
1300 GOTO1700
1400 LET C=A*.07
1600 LET C=A*.10
1700 PRINT S,N$,A,C
1800 LET L=L+1
1900 IF L>10 THEN 100
2000 GOTO 500
2100 PRINT"END OF INPUT"
2200 DATA 100,"J ABEL",500
2300 DATA 115,"S BELL",1500
2400 DATA 119,"A CAVE",2300
2500 DATA 225,"C CHART",3100
2600 DATA 226,"Q CRUZ",1000
2700 DATA 278,"D DE LANE",2000
2800 DATA 305,"F FLIN",3000
2900 DATA 330,"A FULTON",5000
3000 DATA 365,"A GRAY",2300
3100 DATA 400,"L HOBBS",1990
3200 DATA 444,"W LAKELAND",3300
3300 DATA 470,"N PARKER",1999
3400 DATA 500,"R MOORE",4000
3500 DATA 554,"F PRATT",3900
3600 DATA 999,"LAST",0
3700 END
```

FIGURE 7.1a Sales Commission Program with Logic Errors

Upon examination of the program, several errors are noted. The first, labelled (1), shows that Abel has no commission calculated. This could be because of a forgotten calculation or an error relating to the first record into the program. The second error (2) shows incorrect calculations for some of the salesmen. For instance, Cruz's commission should be 70 not 100 dollars. Lastly (3) after 10 lines, a heading is printed for each line although the headings were OK prior to this.

An experienced programmer might be able to find these errors without a trace; however, to show how to use the technique, we will use a trace to assist in discovering the origin of each error.

Since it seems most likely that error 1 is due to a calculation problem, we will insert a statement to determine the result of the calculation. Calculations for amounts that are less than 1000 are done in line 1200. To check the result of this, the following statement is placed after the calculation:

1250 PRINT "<1000 COMMISSION";C

This will tell us the actual computed value.

Problem 2 is an incorrect percentage being applied to the amount. All of these salesmen are in the less than 2000 category.

SALES NO.	NAME	AMOUNT	COMMISSION
100	J ABEL	500	⓪
115	S BELL	1500	150.
119	A CAVE	2300	230.
225	C CHART	3100	372
226	Q CRUZ	1000	100.
278	D DE LANE	2000	200.
305	F FLIN	3000	360
330	A FULTON	5000	600
365	A GRAY	2300	230.
400	L HOBBS	1990	199.
444	W LAKELAND	3300	396

SALES NO.	NAME	AMOUNT	COMMISSION
470	N PARKER	1999	199.9

SALES NO.	NAME	AMOUNT	COMMISSION
500	R MOORE	4000	480

SALES NO.	NAME	AMOUNT	COMMISSION
554	F PRATT	3900	468

SALES NO.	NAME	AMOUNT	COMMISSION

END OF INPUT

FIGURE 7.1b   Sales Commission Program Output

They receive a 7% commission, which is computed by statement 1400. To check this result, the next statement is used:

1500 PRINT" < 2000 COMMISSION";C

The last error is related to the repeating of headings after the tenth line. Since L is used to count lines, it will be printed each time it is incremented. This is done with:

1850 PRINT "LINE COUNT" = ;L

All of these trace statements are included in the next run of the program, as shown in Figure 7.2. To save space, the DATA statements are deleted from this printout although they are still a part of the program. Following the program is the output that we will now consider.

When we examine the results of our trace, we are led to the necessary corrections for the program. The first error we were trying to find was the zero commission for Abel. The trace that was inserted in the program produced no output. This is a strong clue to finding the error; it means that the program never reached statement 1250, the trace. In this case, it also never reached line 1200, which calculates the commission. Therefore, we should check the code that is supposed to bring us here but that failed to do so. This is statement 700, which branches to 1300 if A is less than 1000. The branch should have been to statement 1200 since line 1300 is a GOTO statement.

```
100 REM SALES COMMISSION PROGRAM
200 PRINT
300 PRINT"SALES NO.","NAME","AMOUNT","COMMISSION"
400 PRINT
500 READ S,N$,A
600 IF S=999 THEN 2100
700 IF A<1000 THEN 1300
800 IF A<2000 THEN 1400
900 IF A<3000 THEN 1600
1000 LET C=A*.12
1100 GOTO 1700
1200 LET C=A*.05
1250 PRINT"< 1000 COMMISSION";C
1300 GOTO1700
1400 LET C=A*.07
1500 PRINT"< 2000 COMMISSION";C
1600 LET C=A*.10
1700 PRINT S,N$,A,C
1800 LET L=L+1
1850 PRINT "LINE COUNT =";L
1900 IF L>10 THEN 100
2000 GOTO 500
2100 PRINT"END OF INPUT"
```

Trace
Statements

FIGURE 7.2a   Sales Commission Program with Trace Statements

The program change is made, giving:

700 IF A<1000 THEN 1200

The second error does produce a trace output. It shows that the calculation for Cruz's commission was 70 but that 100 was printed in the report. Thus the calculation is right, but the output is wrong. If we look at this part of the program, we see the 7% is calculated in 1400. The next statement is the trace which is followed by a calculation for 10%. Apparently we forgot the GOTO after 1400. So the trace may

```
SALES NO.              NAME                    AMOUNT              COMMISSION

  100               J ABEL                     500                   0
LINE COUNT = 1                    (2)
< 2000 COMMISSION (105.)
  115               S BELL                    1500                 150.
LINE COUNT = 2
  119               A CAVE                    2300                 230.
LINE COUNT = 3
  225               C CHART                   3100                 372
LINE COUNT = 4                    (2)
< 2000 COMMISSION (70.)
  226               Q CRUZ                    1000                 100.
LINE COUNT = 5
  278               D DE LANE                 2000                 200.
LINE COUNT = 6
  305               F FLIN                    3000                 360
LINE COUNT = 7
  330               A FULTON                  5000                 600
LINE COUNT = 8
  365               A GRAY                    2300                 230.
LINE COUNT = 9
< 2000 COMMISSION 139.3
  400               L HOBBS                   1990                 199.
LINE COUNT = 10
  444               W LAKELAND                3300                 396
LINE COUNT = (11)

SALES NO.              NAME          (3)       AMOUNT              COMMISSION

< 2000 COMMISSION 139.93
  470               N PARKER                  1999                 199.9
LINE COUNT = (12)
                                    (3)
SALES NO.              NAME                    AMOUNT              COMMISSION

  500               R MOORE                   4000                 480
LINE COUNT = 13

SALES NO.              NAME                    AMOUNT              COMMISSION

  554               F PRATT                   3900                 468
LINE COUNT = 14

SALES NO.              NAME                    AMOUNT              COMMISSION

END OF INPUT
```

FIGURE 7.2b   Program and Trace Output

```
100 REM SALES COMMISSION PROGRAM
150 LET L=0
200 PRINT
300 PRINT"SALES NO.","NAME","AMOUNT","COMMISSION"
400 PRINT
500 READ S,N$,A
600 IF S=999 THEN 2100
700 IF A<1000 THEN 1200
800 IF A<2000 THEN 1400
900 IF A<3000 THEN 1600
1000 LET C=A*.12
1100 GOTO 1700
1200 LET C=A*.05
1300 GOTO1700
1400 LET C=A*.07
1500 GOTO 1700
1600 LET C=A*.10
1700 PRINT S,N$,A,C
1800 LET L=L+1
1900 IF L>10 THEN 100
2000 GOTO 500
2100 PRINT"END OF INPUT"
2200 DATA 100,"J ABEL",500
2300 DATA 115,"S BELL",1500
2400 DATA 119,"A CAVE",2300
2500 DATA 225,"C CHART",3100
2600 DATA 226,"Q CRUZ",1000
2700 DATA 278,"D DE LANE",2000
2800 DATA 305,"F FLIN",3000'
2900 DATA 330,"A FULTON",5000
3000 DATA 365,"A GRAY",2300
3100 DATA 400,"L HOBBS",1990
3200 DATA 444,"W LAKELAND",3300
3300 DATA 470,"N PARKER",1999
3400 DATA 500,"R MOORE",4000
3500 DATA 554,"F PRATT",3900
3600 DATA 999,"LAST",0
3700 END
```

SALES NO.	NAME	AMOUNT	COMMISSION
100	J ABEL	500	25
115	S BELL	1500	105.
119	A CAVE	2300	230.
225	C CHART	3100	372
226	Q CRUZ	1000	70.
278	D DE LANE	2000	200.
305	F FLIN	3000	360
330	A FULTON	5000	600
365	A GRAY	2300	230.
400	L HOBBS	1990	139.3
444	W LAKELAND	3300	396

SALES NO.	NAME	AMOUNT	COMMISSION
470	N PARKER	1999	139.93
500	R MOORE	4000	480
554	F PRATT	3900	468

END OF INPUT

FIGURE 7.3 Sales Commission Program—Debugged

be replaced by:

1500 GOTO 1700

The heading error also gives some interesting and useful output. The line counter L continues to increase in value after the second heading is printed. Therefore, each time that the program comes to 1900, the variable L is always greater than 10, and a heading is printed. To correct this, it is necessary to ensure that L is set back to zero when a heading is printed. This can be done by inserting:

150 LET L = 0

Now we remove all trace statements and rerun the program for a final test run as shown in Figure 7.3.

8
Subscripted Variables, Arrays and Matrix Commands

When a large volume of data is handled, it is quite cumbersome to write a program to access each value with a different variable name. An array, or table, is normally used to facilitate the storage and use of such a set of values. The array is given a name, one of the valid variable names in BASIC, and the various values stored are accessed by that variable name combined with a subscript. The subscript is a number, or numeric variable, that is enclosed in parentheses and appears after the array name. Such a combination might be:

$$C(6)$$

where C is the array name and 6 is the subscript. If 20 values are to be stored under the variable name C, the subscript could be any integer from 1 to 20, or it could be a numeric variable with a value in the proper range (1 to 20). Thus, the following statements could be used to access one of the values in the array called C.

```
70   LET I=4
80   PRINT C(I)
```

These instructions cause the value in C(4) to be printed.

SETTING UP THE ARRAY—
THE DIM STATEMENT

If an array is required to store more than 10 values, most BASIC systems require that the number of values be defined in a DIM statement (dimension). Up to 10 values may be assigned and used without defining the array.

The general format of the DIM statement is shown in Figure 8.1. The constant in Figure 8.1 defines the number of storage locations, or the number of values to be stored under that array name.

The DIM statement may be located anywhere in a program; however, on some systems, it must precede the actual use of the array. A single DIM statement may be used to define the dimensions of more than one array. The number of values to be stored must be specified as a numeric constant. If the exact number is not known,

---

statement number   DIM   array name (constant), array name (constant),...

FIGURE 8.1   DIM Statement—General Format

the maximum number expected should be specified, with any excess storage locations left unused.

EXAMPLES

Example 1:   Storing Values in Arrays

If we wished to store 15 data items in an array, 15 storage locations would be requested in a DIM statement. The following program sets up such a table, reads 15 data items into the array and prints the contents of the array.

```
00010 DIM A(15)
00020 FOR I=1 TO 15
00030 READ A(I)
00040 NEXT I
00050 FOR I=1 TO 15
00060 PRINT A(I);
00070 NEXT I
00080 DATA 30,6,45,12,75,342,67,1,93,204,62,54,96,61,85
00090 END
 30   6   45   12   75   342   67   1   93   204   62   54   96   61   85
```

The FOR—NEXT loops control both the reading and printing of the data. In the first loop, the value of I is set at 1 by the FOR statement, and the first execution of the READ statement results in a value being assigned to A(1). The FOR—NEXT loop causes the READ statement to be executed again and again, increasing the value of I by 1 each time and placing a value in A(2), A(3), . . . A(15). The second loop causes the repetition of the PRINT statement 15 times, with the value of I again going from 1 to 15. The contents of all 15 storage locations are thus printed.

```
00010 DIM A(15)
00020 FOR I=1 TO 15
00030 READ A(I)
00040 NEXT I
00050 FOR I=1 TO 15
00060 PRINT A(I)
00070 NEXT I
00080 DATA 30,6,45,12,75,342,67,1,93,204,62,54,96,61,35
00090 END
 30
 6
 45
 12
 75
 342
 67
 1
 93
 204
 62
 54
 96
 61
 85
```

The semicolon at the end of line 60 causes the printing to be done on the same line. If the semicolon were removed, the output would be written down the page in a column, as shown above.

Example 2: Finding Averages With Arrays

This program reads and stores 12 data values in an array and prints the 12 values. The numbers in the array are not destroyed by printing. The program then determines the average of the stored numbers by adding them to a total and then dividing the total by 12. The average is printed by statement 140.

```
00010 DIM N(15)
00020 FOR A=1 TO 15
00030 READ N(A)
00040 NEXT A
00050 PRINT "THE VALUES IN THE ARRAY ARE"
00060 PRINT
00070 FOR A=1 TO 15
00080 PRINT N(A);
00090 NEXT A
00100 LET S=N(1)
00110 FOR A=1 TO 15
00120 IF N(A)<S THEN 140
00130 LET S=N(A)
00140 NEXT A
00150 PRINT
00160 PRINT
00170 PRINT "THE LARGEST NUMBER IS ";S
00180 DATA 45,876,835,536,489,947,3648,544,3,76,9,456,867,24,64
00190 END

THE VALUES IN THE ARRAY ARE

 45   876   835   536   489   947   3648   544   3   76   9   456   867   24   64

THE LARGEST NUMBER IS  3648
```

Example 3: Searching For Largest or Smallest Value

This program reads 15 numbers, stores them in an array, prints the contents of the array, finds the largest number in the table, and prints it.

```
00010 DIM C(12)
00020 FOR A=1 TO 12
00030 READ C(A)
00040 NEXT A
00050 FOR A=1 TO 12
00060 PRINT C(A);
00070 NEXT A
00080 FOR A=1 TO 12
00090 LET T=T+C(A)
00100 NEXT A
00110 LET N=T/12
00120 PRINT
00130 PRINT
00140 PRINT "THE AVERAGE IS ";N
00150 DATA 65,86,59,90,75,79,48,67,71,64,83,78
00160 END

 65   86   59   90   75   79   48   67   71   64   83   78

THE AVERAGE IS  72.03333
```

SOME MATRIX OPERATIONS

At this point, it is useful to illustrate the matrix, an alternate method of controlling the reading and writing of an array. As has been shown in the Examples 1-3, these operations may be easily controlled by the FOR—NEXT loop. Since the matrix operations are not available on all BASIC systems, it may be necessary to continue with this method on your particular system. Most systems, however, do offer the matrix facility.

The word matrix is technically only applied to two dimensional arrays. (Two dimensional arrays are covered later in this chapter.) In BASIC, however, any array may be manipulated by statements with the MAT option.

The use of the MAT option is basically intended to relieve the programmer of the task of controlling a subscript when it is necessary to perform some common operations on an array. This includes reading data and storing the values in an array, printing the contents of an array or performing some specific calculations on the values in an array. The MAT option may be specified for the READ, INPUT, PRINT and LET statements.

The following programs show how the MAT option could be used in Examples 1, 2 and 3. The program from Example 1 could be written as follows.

```
00010 DIM A(15)
00020 MAT READ A
00030 MAT PRINT A;
00040 DATA 30,6,45,12,75,342,67,1,93,204,62,54,96,61,85
00050 END
30   6   45   12   75   342   67   1   93   204   62   54   96   61   85
```

Or, if a column of numbers is required, the semicolon may be removed.

```
00010 DIM A(15)
00020 MAT READ A
00030 MAT PRINT A
00040 DATA 30,6,45,12,75,342,67,1,93,204,62,54,96,61,85
00050 END
30
6
45
12
75
342
67
1
93
204
62
54
96
61
85
```

Example 2 could be shortened to the following:

```
00010 DIM C(12)
00020 MAT READ C
00030 MAT PRINT C;
00040 FOR A=1 TO 12
00050 LET T=T+C(A)
00060 NEXT A
00070 LET N=T/12
00080 PRINT
00090 PRINT "THE AVERAGE IS ";N
00100 DATA 65,86,59,90,75,79,48,67,71,64,83,78
00110 END
```
```
65   86   59   90   75   79   48   67   71   64   83   78

THE AVERAGE IS   72.08333
```

Example 3, using the MAT option, looks like this:

```
00010 DIM N(15)
00020 MAT READ N
00030 PRINT "THE VALUES IN THE ARRAY ARE"
00040 MAT PRINT N;
00050 LET S=N(1)
00060 FOR A=1 TO 15
00070 IF N(A)<S THEN 90
00080 LET S=N(A)
00090 NEXT A
00100 PRINT
00110 PRINT "THE LARGEST NUMBER IS ";S
00120 DATA 45,876,935,536,489,947,3648,544,3,76,9,456,867,24,64
00130 END
```
```
THE VALUES IN THE ARRAY ARE

 45   876   935   536   489   947   3648   544   3   76   9   456   867   24   64

THE LARGEST NUMBER IS   3648
```

In the READ statement, the MAT option may redefine the size of the array given in the DIM statement. The following program shows an array defined with 25 elements in the DIM statement, but, since there are only 15 data items, the READ statement changes the definition to 15. Notice that the MAT option in the PRINT statement maintains the most recent definition.

```
00010 DIM G(25)
00020 MAT READ G(15)
00030 MAT PRINT G
00040 DATA 60,70,65,80,56,78,67,84,98,59
00050 DATA 58,79,86,78,81
00060 END
60
70
65
80
56
78
67
84
98
59
58
79
86
78
81
```

The net effect of the MAT READ and MAT PRINT statements is that the FOR—NEXT statements need not be written. The values will be read from the DATA statement(s) and written from the storage locations without being specifically identified by the programmer in a normal READ or PRINT statement. If the data is to be supplied from the keyboard rather than from DATA statements, MAT INPUT may be used. This feature is covered later in the chapter along with some additional matrix operations.

SORTING VALUES IN AN ARRAY

Sorting, or arranging values in sequence, is a common requirement in computer programming. Several programs illustrate different sorting techniques.

Sorting a set of numbers usually requires that several "passes" or iterations be made through the logic. In the illustrations that follow, the contents of the array are printed twice, once before the sort begins and once after all iterations have been made. At this point, the numbers in the array are in sequence. It is assumed that an ascending sequence is required, though values could as easily be arranged in descending order.

THE BUBBLE SORT

One sorting technique is called a "bubble sort" in that, just as bubbles rise in water, the program carries the largest values toward the end of the table and thus arranges them in order. The following program is an example of a bubble sort.

```
00010 DIM N(12)
00020 MAT READ N
00030 PRINT "THIS IS THE ARRAY IN RANDOM SEQUENCE"
00040 MAT PRINT N;
00050 FOR Y=1 TO 11
00060 FOR X=1 TO 11
00070 IF N(X)<=N(X+1) THEN 110
00080 LET H=N(X)
00090 LET N(X)=N(X+1)
00100 LET N(X+1)=H
00110 NEXT X
00120 NEXT Y
00130 PRINT
00140 PRINT "THIS IS THE SORTED ARRAY"
00150 MAT PRINT N;
00160 DATA 3462,2807,3528,7352,5481,683,6286,9578,24,8235,452,4623
00170 END

THIS IS THE ARRAY IN RANDOM SEQUENCE

 3462  2807  3528  7352  5481   683  6286  9578    24  8235   452  4623

THIS IS THE SORTED ARRAY

   24   452   683  2807  3462  3528  4623  5481  6286  7352  8235  9578
```

The following program is also a bubble sort, but it has been altered to show the changes made by each pass through the table. Notice that the larger values are carried toward the end of the array, and the smaller numbers are displaced toward the beginning.

```
00010 DIM N(12)
00020 MAT READ N
00030 PRINT "THIS IS THE ARRAY IN RANDOM SEQUENCE"
00040 MAT PRINT N;
00050 FOR Y=1 TO 11
00060 FOR X=1 TO 11
00070 IF N(X)<=N(X+1) THEN 120
00080 LET S=1
00090 LET H=N(X)
00100 LET N(X)=N(X+1)
00110 LET N(X+1)=H
00120 NEXT X
00130 IF S=0 THEN 190
00140 LET S=0
00150 PRINT
00160 PRINT "AFTER PASS ";Y
00170 MAT PRINT N;
00180 NEXT Y
00190 PRINT
00200 PRINT "THIS IS THE SORTED ARRAY"
00210 MAT PRINT N;
00220 DATA 3462,2807,3528,7352,5481,683,6286,9578,24,8235,452,4623
00230 END
```

The variable S is given the value 1 when two numbers are switched so that the larger one is moved toward the end. It is returned to the value 0 (zero) after a complete pass has been made

```
THIS IS THE ARRAY IN RANDOM SEQUENCE
 3462  2807  3528  7352  5481   683  6286  9578    24  8235   452  4623
AFTER PASS  1
 2807  3462  3528  5481   683  6286  7352    24  8235   452  4623  9578
AFTER PASS  2
 2807  3462  3528   683  5481  6286    24  7352   452  4623  8235  9578
AFTER PASS  3
 2807  3462   683  3528  5481    24  6286   452  4623  7352  8235  9578
AFTER PASS  4
 2807   683  3462  3528    24  5481   452  4623  6286  7352  8235  9578
AFTER PASS  5
  683  2807  3462    24  3528   452  4623  5481  6286  7352  8235  9578
AFTER PASS  6
  683  2807    24  3462   452  3528  4623  5481  6286  7352  8235  9578
AFTER PASS  7
  683    24  2807   452  3462  3528  4623  5481  6286  7352  8235  9578
AFTER PASS  8
   24   683   452  2807  3462  3528  4623  5481  6286  7352  8235  9578
AFTER PASS  9
   24   452   683  2807  3462  3528  4623  5481  6286  7352  8235  9578
THIS IS THE SORTED ARRAY
   24   452   683  2807  3462  3528  4623  5481  6286  7352  8235  9578
```

through the elements of the array. If the value of S is 0 after all elements of the array have been checked, then there were no changes made; since the numbers are now all in order, there is no need to continue. Statement 130 sends control out of the sort loop to statement 190 when this occurs.

The following program is also a sort. This time, two FOR—NEXT loops are used to bring the smallest value to the beginning of the array. As the numbers are arranged in sequence, the list of unsorted numbers becomes smaller. The outer loop controls a variable whose value indicates the position that will contain the next smallest value in the table. On the first pass through the logic, the value of A is 1, and the smallest number is placed in the first position. The value of A then becomes 2, and the next smallest number is stored in the second position after all the remaining 9 values have been checked. As the value of A increases, the smaller values are not considered in the search for the value that should be next in the sequence. When the value of A is 10, all numbers have been arranged in order, and the sequenced values are printed.

```
00010 DIM N(12)
00020 MAT READ N
00030 PRINT
00040 PRINT "THIS IS THE ARRAY IN RANDOM SEQUENCE"
00050 MAT PRINT N;
00060 FOR A=1 TO 12
00070 FOR B=1 TO 12
00080 IF N(A)>N(B) THEN 120
00090 LET H=N(A)
00100 LET N(A)=N(B)
00110 LET N(B)=H
00120 NEXT B
00130 NEXT A
00140 PRINT
00150 PRINT "THIS IS THE SORTED ARRAY"
00160 MAT PRINT N;
00170 DATA 3462,2807,3528,7352,5481,683,6286,9578,24,8235,452,4623
00180 END
```

```
THIS IS THE ARRAY IN RANDOM SEQUENCE

 3462  2807  3528  7352  5481   683  6286  9578    24  8235   452  4623

THIS IS THE SORTED ARRAY

  24   452   683  2807  3462  3528  4623  5481  6286  7352  8235  9578
```

SORTING ALPHANUMERIC DATA

As indicated in Chapter 6, alphanumeric data may be compared, and therefore it can be arranged in alphabetical order. The following program is a sort, but it is intended to arrange alphanumeric data in order.

```
00010 DIM N$(10)
00020 MAT READ N$
00030 PRINT "THE NAMES WERE READ IN THIS ORDER"
00040 MAT PRINT N$
00050 REM - SORT THE NAMES IN ALPHABETICAL ORDER
00060 FOR I=1 TO 10
00070 FOR J=I TO 10
00080 IF N$(I)<N$(J) THEN 120
00090 LET H$=N$(I)
00100 LET N$(I)=N$(J)
00110 LET N$(J)=H$
00120 NEXT J
00130 NEXT I
00140 PRINT "THE NAMES ARE NOW IN ALPHABETICAL ORDER"
00150 MAT PRINT N$
00160 DATA JONES,BROWN,MONTGOMERY,THOMAS,SMITH
00170 DATA GREEN,VANDERWEL,IRWIN,THOMPSON,ADAMS
00180 END


THE NAMES WERE READ IN THIS ORDER

JONES
BROWN
MONTGOMERY
THOMAS
SMITH
GREEN
VANDERWEL
IRWIN
THOMPSON
ADAMS

THE NAMES ARE NOW IN ALPHABETICAL ORDER

ADAMS
BROWN
GREEN
IRWIN
JONES
MONTGOMERY
SMITH
THOMAS
THOMPSON
VANDERWEL
```

USING PART OF AN ARRAY

In some problems, the exact number of values to be stored in an array is not known. For example, if it were necessary to store the marks achieved by a class of students, how many locations are necessary to hold a grade for each student? Does every class always have the same number of students?

In a case like this, we require a definition of the number of students that could reasonably be expected in a class. Let us assume that there will never be more than 40 students in any class. The dimension defined in the DIM statement would then be 40. Are there 40 students in every class? Probably not. How could this be programmed? In Example 4, the last grade in the data is 999. This is used as the indicator that no more data is available and that the program can proceed to work on the 30 data items (marks), which have been stored, without accessing the last 10 elements of the array, which have not been assigned values.

Example 4

Read in the grades of all students in a class. Print the grades. Print the highest grade, the lowest grade and the class average. There are no more than 40 students in the class; the last grade is recognized when 999 is read.

The program logic is divided into modules, each of which is responsible for performing one function. The first module reads the data and stores it in the array, the second prints the grades, etc. Each module uses a FOR—NEXT loop to step through the array to perform its particular function.

```
00010 DIM G(40)
00020 REM - READ IN THE GRADES
00030 FOR K=1 TO 40
00040 READ G(K)
00050 IF G(K)=999 THEN 70
00060 GO TO 90
00070 LET J=K-1
00080 LET K=40
00090 NEXT K
00100 REM - PRINT THE GRADES
00110 FOR K= 1 TO J
00120 PRINT G(K);
00130 NEXT K
00140 REM - FIND THE HIGHEST GRADE
00150 LET L=G(1)
00160 FOR K=1 TO J
00170 IF L>G(K) THEN 190
00180 LET L=G(K)
00190 NEXT K
00200 REM - FIND THE LOWEST GRADE
00210 LET S=G(1)
00220 FOR K=1 TO J
00230 IF S<G(K) THEN 250
00240 LET S=G(K)
00250 NEXT K
00260 REM - FIND THE CLASS AVERAGE
00270 LET T=0
00280 FOR K=1 TO J
00290 LET T=T+G(K)
00300 NEXT K
00310 LET A=T/J
00320 PRINT
00330 PRINT
00340 PRINT "THE HIGHEST GRADE IN THE CLASS IS ";L
00350 PRINT
00360 PRINT "THE LOWEST GRADE IN THE CLASS IS ";S
00370 PRINT
```

```
00380 PRINT "THE CLASS AVERAGE IS ";A
00390 DATA 78,46,54,97,65
00400 DATA 66,23,77,56,83
00410 DATA 73,92,84,54,35
00420 DATA 86,89,75,78,68
00430 DATA 98,67,98,45,76
00440 DATA 80,65,59,90,999
00450 END
```

```
78  46  54  97  65  66  23  77  56  83  73  92  84  54  35  86  89  75
78  68  88  67  98  45  76  80  65  59  90
```

```
THE HIGHEST GRADE IN THE CLASS IS  98

THE LOWEST GRADE IN THE CLASS IS  23

THE CLASS AVERAGE IS  70.58621
```

LOGICALLY RELATED DATA

If the program in Example 4 were required to identify the student who had achieved the highest or lowest grade, it would have to be modified to accept and store the students' identification as well as their grades. This can be accomplished easily by storing the student names in one array and the grades in another. The alphabetic data may be stored in an array by using an alphanumeric data name and defining its dimension in a DIM statement. The names and grades can be matched: the first grade is stored in G(1) while the name of the student who achieved that grade is stored in N$(1). Note that the subscripts are the same. This method of storage could be depicted by the following diagram.

Array N$		Array G
G. SMITH	—(1)—	73
N. COLE	—(2)—	64
A. CHAPMAN	—(3)—	86
D. GROVE	—(4)—	85
T. PIRRI	—(5)—	80
—	—	—
—	—	—
—	—	—

The name, with a particular subscript, achieved a grade, with the same subscript. In the above illustration, D. GROVE achieved a grade of 85; N$(4) would thus have a grade of G(4).

Example 5

Read and store the name and grade of each student in a class. Print an honor list, i.e. people who achieved 75% or more. Print the name and grade of the student with the highest grade. There are no more than 40 students.

```
00010 DIM N$(40),G(40)
00020 FOR I=1 TO 40
00030 READ N$(I),G(I)
00040 IF G(I)=999 THEN 60
00050 GO TO 80
00060 LET J=I-1
00070 LET I=40
00080 NEXT I
00090 PRINT
00100 PRINT "THE HONOUR STUDENTS ARE"
00110 PRINT
00120 FOR I= 1 TO J
00130 IF G(I)<75 THEN 150
00140 PRINT N$(I),G(I)
00150 NEXT I
00160 LET L=G(1)
00170 FOR I=1 TO J
00180 IF G(I)<L THEN 210
00190 LET S$=N$(I)
00200 LET L=G(I)
00210 NEXT I
00220 PRINT
00230 PRINT "THE STUDENT WTH THE HIGHEST GRADE IS"
00240 PRINT
00250 PRINT S$;" WHO ACHIEVED";L;"PERCENT"
00260 DATA T. GRAY,72
00270 DATA A. PARWITZ,81
00280 DATA N. JOHNSON,68
00290 DATA D. ALTOZE,90
00300 DATA L. NORTHEY,85
00310 DATA B. RADCLIFFE,79
00320 DATA V. DRAY,96
00330 DATA H. PARR,88
00340 DATA E. PAREZI,60
00350 DATA O. FAULKNER,76
00360 DATA D. COOK,75
00370 DATA S. MARTIN,88
00380 DATA S. BENNETTO,74
00390 DATA G. MCLEOD,98
00400 DATA Y. DUREAU,57
00410 DATA T. BARKER,62
00420 DATA P. JORDAN,35
00430 DATA N. DELTO,68
00440 DATA F. SELDERS,80
00450 DATA LAST,999
00460 END
```

```
THE HONOUR STUDENTS ARE

A. PARWITZ      81
D. ALTOZE       90
L. NORTHEY      85
B. RADCLIFFE    79
V. DRAY         96
H. PARR         88
O. FAULKNER     76
```

```
D. COOK           75
S. MARTIN         88
G. MCLEOD         98
F. SELDERS        80
```

THE STUDENT WTH THE HIGHEST GRADE IS

G. MCLEOD WHO ACHIEVED 98 PERCENT

TWO-DIMENSIONAL ARRAYS

A two-dimensional array is defined by a DIM statement in which the array name is given in two dimensions, such as the following:

10   DIM   A(3,4)

In this description, the array name is A, and it is defined as having 3 rows and 4 columns. It could be depicted as follows:

	1	2	3	4
1				
2				
3				

Here, the array is shown with the subscripts in each block.

(1,1)	(1,2)	(1,3)	(1,4)
(2,1)	(2,2)	(2,3)	(2,4)
(3,1)	(3,2)	(3,3)	(3,4)

Note that the first subscript refers to the number of rows in the array whereas the second defines the number of columns. In this case, there are 3 rows of 4 elements, or 12 elements in all.

Each element can be accessed by using the array name with the subscripts enclosed in parentheses in the same fashion as a one-dimensional array. The statement:

$$50 \quad \text{LET } A(2,4)=17$$

assigns a value to one of the elements. If no other assignments have been made, the array would have the following values.

0	0	0	0
0	0	0	17
0	0	0	0

Values for the elements of a two-dimensional array may also be assigned from DATA statements.

Example 6

Read in 12 values and store them in a two-dimensional array with 3 rows and 4 columns. Print the contents of the array.

```
00010 DIM T(3,4)
00020 FOR A=1 TO 3
00030 FOR B=1 TO 4
00040 READ T(A,B)
00050 NEXT B
00060 NEXT A
00070 FOR A=1 TO 3
00080 FOR B=1 TO 4
00090 PRINT T(A,B);
00100 NEXT B
00110 PRINT
00120 NEXT A
00130 DATA 4,2,3,8,9,5,1,7,2,6,5,3
00140 END
```

```
4  2  3  8
9  5  1  7
2  6  5  3
```

MAT READ AND MAT PRINT

The MAT operations may be used to facilitate the reading and printing of two-dimensional arrays, thus relieving the programmer of the task of setting up the proper loops. The definition of the array is "remembered" by the program when the MAT operations of READ and PRINT are performed; therefore, the proper number of values, in this case 12, are read and placed in the array.

The following program illustrates the use of the MAT operations in reading and printing 12 values. Notice how much shorter this program is than the one in Example 6 though the two programs produce the same result from identical data. (Note that some systems do not require a semicolon in MAT PRINT.)

```
00010   DIM T(3,4)
00020   MAT READ T
00030   MAT PRINT T;
00040   DATA 4,2,3,8,9,5,1,7,2,6,5,3
00050   END
4   2   3   8
9   5   1   7
2   6   5   3
```

ADDITIONAL MATRIX OPERATIONS

On many BASIC systems, it is possible to have operations performed on each element of an array. For example, each element of an array may be set to zero or to one. The values in one table may be assigned to another. The following is a summary of the matrix operations.

ZER   sets each element of an array to zero.

```
00010   DIM A(5,3)
00020   MAT A=ZER
00030   MAT PRINT A;
00040   END
0   0   0
0   0   0
0   0   0
0   0   0
0   0   0
```

CON   sets each element of an array to one.

```
00010  DIM A(3,5)
00020  MAT A=CON
00030  MAT PRINT A;
00040  END
```

```
1  1  1  1  1
1  1  1  1  1
1  1  1  1  1
```

Calculations may be performed on each element of an array; addition, subtraction or multiplication may be specified. The following programs show the results of addition and multiplication.

ADDITION

```
00010 DIM C(4,3),X(4,3),Y(4,3)
00020 MAT READ C
00030 MAT READ X
00040 MAT Y=C+X
00050 PRINT
00060 PRINT "THIS IS THE ARRAY C"
00070 MAT PRINT C;
00080 PRINT
00090 PRINT "THIS IS THE ARRAY X"
00100 MAT PRINT X;
00110 PRINT
00120 PRINT "AFTER THE ADDITION OF STATEMENT 40, THIS IS ARRAY Y"
00130 MAT PRINT Y;
00140 DATA 10,20,30,40,50,60,70,80,90,100,110,120
00150 DATA 1,2,3,4,5,6,7,8,9,10,11,12
```

```
THIS IS THE ARRAY C

 10   20   30
 40   50   60
 70   80   90
100  110  120


THIS IS THE ARRAY X

 1   2   3
 4   5   6
 7   8   9
10  11  12


AFTER THE ADDITION OF STATEMENT 40, THIS IS ARRAY Y

 11   22   33
 44   55   66
 77   88   99
110  121  132
```

MULTIPLICATION

```
00010 DIM C(4,3),X(4,3)
00020 MAT READ C
00030 MAT X=(3)*C
00040 PRINT
00050 PRINT "THIS IS THE ARRAY C"
00060 MAT PRINT C;
00070 PRINT "AFTER THE MULTIPLICATION OF STATEMENT 40,"
00080 PRINT "THIS IS ARRAY X"
00090 MAT PRINT X;
00100 DATA 10,20,30,40,50,60,70,80,90,100,110,120
00110 END


THIS IS THE ARRAY C

 10   20   30
 40   50   60
 70   80   90
 100  110  120

AFTER THE MULTIPLICATION OF STATEMENT 40,
THIS IS ARRAY X

 30   60   90
 120  150  180
 210  240  270
 300  330  360
```

INPUT   as mentioned earlier in the chapter, the values to be stored in an array may be entered at the time that the program is run.

```
00010 DIM A(2,3)
00020 PRINT
00030 PRINT "TYPE IN 6 NUMBERS TO STORE IN THE ARRAY"
00040 MAT INPUT A
00050 PRINT
00060 PRINT "THE ARRAY CONTAINS THESE VALUES"
00070 MAT PRINT A;
00080 END


TYPE IN 6 NUMBERS TO STORE IN THE ARRAY
? 32,88,7,14,61,57

THE ARRAY CONTAINS THESE VALUES

 32   88   7
 14   61   57
```

IDN   establishes an identity matrix. An identity matrix is a two-dimensional array with ones along a diagonal and zeros in all other positions.

```
00010 DIM D(6,6)
00020 MAT D=IDN
00030 PRINT
00040 PRINT "THIS IS AN EXAMPLE OF AN IDENTITY MATRIX"
00050 PRINT
00060 PRINT "THE DIAGONAL OF THE ARRAY CONTAINS 1'S, THE REST 0'S"
00070 MAT PRINT D;
00080 END
```

```
THIS IS AN EXAMPLE OF AN IDENTITY MATRIX

THE DIAGONAL OF THE ARRAY CONTAINS 1'S, THE REST 0'S

 1  0  0  0  0  0
 0  1  0  0  0  0
 0  0  1  0  0  0
 0  0  0  1  0  0
 0  0  0  0  1  0
 0  0  0  0  0  1
```

The following matrix operations are of primary interest to mathematicians. They are shown here simply to document their existence.

INV calculates a matrix inversion.

```
00010 DIM M(4,4),N(4,4)
00020 MAT READ M
00030 PRINT
00040 PRINT
00050 PRINT "THE ARRAY CONTAINS THESE VALUES"
00060 MAT PRINT M;
00070 MAT N=INV(M)
00080 PRINT
00090 PRINT "AFTER INVERSION, THE ARRAY LOOKS LIKE THIS"
00100 MAT PRINT N;
00110 DATA 3,54,12,7,17,20,5,8,2,14,50,1,9,10,4,13
00120 END
```

```
THE ARRAY CONTAINS THESE VALUES

 3  54  12   7
17  20   5   8
 2  14  50   1
 9  10   4  13


AFTER INVERSION, THE ARRAY LOOKS LIKE THIS

-0.02386723   0.08335016   0.0004712852 -0.03847707
 0.02064959   0.003815166 -0.004286452 -0.01313708
-0.004869948 -0.003209228  0.02125272   0.002962364
 0.002137615 -0.05965125  -0.003568303  0.112755
```

TRN is used to transpose the values in a two-dimensional array.
The rows become columns and vice versa.

```
00010 DIM T(4,3),R(3,4)
00020 MAT READ T
00030 PRINT
00040 PRINT "THE ARRAY CONTAINS THESE VALUES "
00050 MAT PRINT T;
00060 MAT R=TRN(T)
00070 PRINT
00080 PRINT "THE TRANSPOSED ARRAY LOOKS LIKE THIS"
00090 MAT PRINT R;
00100 DATA 13,7,4,15,10,11,3,8,14,9,2,5
00110 END
```

```
THE ARRAY CONTAINS THESE VALUES

13   7   4
15  10  11
 3   8  14
 9   2   5


THE TRANSPOSED ARRAY LOOKS LIKE THIS

13  15   3   9
 7  10   8   2
 4  11  14   5
```

AVERAGING GRADES BY STUDENT AND COURSE

There is a class of students, each of whom has taken five
subjects. Each data record contains a student's name and the
grades achieved in the five subjects. There are no more than 25
students, but there may be less. The end of the data is marked by a
data record with the name "LAST."

A list is required showing each student's grades along with
his/her average. The report also shows the course averages. After all
averages have been calculated, print out all the information.

In the solution to this problem, four arrays are used: student
names(N$), student grades (G), student averages (S) and course
averages (C).

```
00010 DIM N$(25),G(25,5),S(25),C(5)
00020 REM --
00030 REM -- THE TWO FOR-NEXT LOOPS READ ALL THE STUDENT DATA
00040 REM -- AND STORE THE NAMES AND GRADES IN THE ARRAYS N$ AND G.
00050 REM --
00060 FOR I=1 TO 25
00070 READ N$(I)
00080 IF N$(I)><"LAST" THEN 120
00090 K=I-1
00100 I=25
00110 GO TO 150
00120 FOR J=1 TO 5
00130 READ G(I,J)
00140 NEXT J
00150 NEXT I
00160 REM --
00170 REM -- THE FOLLOWING INSTRUCTIONS CALCULATE THE STUDENT AVERAGE
00180 REM -- WHICH ARE STORED IN THE ARRAY S
00190 REM --
00200 FOR I=1 TO K
00210 T=0
00220 FOR J=1 TO 5
00230 T=T+G(I,J)
00240 NEXT J
00250 S(I)=T/5
00260 NEXT I
00270 REM --
00280 REM -- THESE INSTRUCTIONS CALCULATE THE COURSE AVERAGES
00290 REM -- WHICH ARE STORED IN THE ARRAY C
00300 REM --
00310 FOR J=1 TO 5
00320 T=0
00330 FOR I=1 TO K
00340 T=T+G(I,J)
00350 NEXT I
00360 C(J)=T/K
00370 NEXT J
00380 PRINT
00390 REM --
00400 REM -- THESE INSTRUCTIONS PRINT THE HEADINGS
00410 REM --
00420 PRINT USING 430,
00430:      NAME                STUDENT  GRADES                    AVERAGE
00440 PRINT USING 450,
00450:                    1     2     3     4     5
00460 REM --
00470 REM -- ALL DATA IS PRINTED BY THE FOLLOWING INSTRUCTIONS
00480 REM --
00490 FOR I=1 TO K
00500 PRINT USING 510,N$(I);
00510:    'LLLLLLLLLL
00520 FOR J=1 TO 5
00530 PRINT USING 540,G(I,J);
00540:     ###
00550 NEXT J
00560 PRINT USING 570,S(I)
00570:    ####.#
00580 NEXT I
00590 PRINT USING 600,
00600:    COURSE
00610 PRINT USING 620,A$;
00620:    AVERAGES'L
00630 FOR J=1 TO 5
00640 PRINT USING 650,C(J);
00650: ###.#
00660 NEXT J
00670 PRINT
00680 PRINT
```

```
00690 DATA R. LOCKHART,95,89,91,94,90
00700 DATA A. BOTHWICK,79,81,76,84,80
00710 DATA W. WILSON, 75,60,68,72,64
00720 DATA G. PARELLI,59,63,70,60,58
00730 DATA A. SINGH,50,58,61,49,57
00740 DATA G. FRANKLIN,66,70,68,74,71
00750 DATA J. CARLOS,82,70,79,74,80
00760 DATA J. ANDERSON,58,80,76,82,70
00770 DATA G. SIDEY,92,84,88,79,87
00780 DATA T. VAN HORN,74,78,65,73,69
00790 DATA L. DALEY,84,80,82,87,89
00800 DATA S. MAGILL,52,60,58,64,48
00810 DATA G. REED,45,51,58,49,40
00820 DATA R. COLE,68,62,59,70,64
00830 DATA D. SPRAGG,82,86,80,79,90
00840 DATA T. BURNS,74,72,64,74,76
00850 DATA P. ANDREWS,69,73,68,72,74
00860 DATA F. MITCHELL,70,80,78,81,76
00870 DATA L. GRANT,47,75,68,71,59
00880 DATA D. LEWITT,59,63,60,68,65
00390 DATA J. MCDONALD,94,97,88,93,91
00900 DATA K. BLAIR,82,80,84,78,85
00910 DATA LAST,9,9,9,9,9
00920 END
```

NAME	STUDENT		GRADES			AVERAGE
	1	2	3	4	5	
R. LOCKHART	95	89	91	94	90	91.8
A. BOTHWICK	79	81	76	84	80	80.0
W. WILSON	75	60	68	72	64	67.8
G. PARELLI	59	63	70	60	58	62.0
A. SINGH	50	58	61	49	57	55.0
G. FRANKLIN	66	70	68	74	71	69.8
J. CARLOS	82	70	79	74	80	77.0
J. ANDERSON	58	80	76	82	70	73.2
G. SIDEY	92	84	88	79	87	86.0
T. VAN HORN	74	78	65	73	69	71.8
L. DALEY	84	80	82	87	89	84.4
S. MAGILL	52	60	58	64	48	56.4
G. REED	45	51	58	49	40	48.6
R. COLE	68	62	59	70	64	64.6
D. SPRAGG	82	86	80	79	90	83.4
T. BURNS	74	72	64	74	76	72.0
P. ANDREWS	69	73	68	72	74	71.2
F. MITCHELL	70	80	78	81	76	77.0
L. GRANT	47	75	68	71	59	64.0
D. LEWITT	59	63	60	68	65	63.0
J. MCDONALD	94	97	88	93	91	92.6
K. BLAIR	82	80	84	78	85	81.8
COURSE AVERAGES	70.7	73.3	72.2	74.0	72.0	

COMMON ERRORS

1.
```
10  FOR N=1 TO 20
20  LET A(N)=N
30  NEXT N
```

The upper bound (number of elements) of the array has not been defined in a DIM statement. A table containing more than 10 elements must be defined. *Correction:* 5   DIM A(20)

2.   10   DIM X(15)
       20   READ X
       30

If it is the intent of statement 20 to fill the array, it will not work. The variable X is recognized as being distinct from X(?), where the ? is any subscript. Thus, X and X(1) are not connected in any way unless the MAT operation is specified.
Correction: 20   MAT READ X

3.   10   DIM K(15)
       20   LET K3=62

The variable K3 is not part of the array K. If the 3 is intended as a subscript, it must be enclosed in parentheses.
Correction: 20   LET K(3)=62

4.   10   DIM A(12)
       20   LET A(15)=15

The upper bound of the array A has been defined by the DIM statement as 12. The subscript 15 is therefore not valid.
Correction: use subscripts within the valid range.

5.   10   DIM Z(K)

The number of elements intended for this array must be defined as a number. If the value of K is defined before statement 10, the DIM statement, BASIC can reserve the proper number of storage locations. The number of elements may be changed following the DIM statement only by the MAT READ, MAT ZER, MAT CON and MAT IDN statements.

6.   10   DIM J(4000000)

The number of elements in one dimension is limited. Different systems have different maxima, so the one shown here may be valid on some systems. The documentation for your particular machine should be consulted.

QUESTIONS

1.   Identify the errors in each of the following statements.

    a)   10 MAT READ A
               20 MAT PRINT A
               30 DATA 6,2,9,4,3,0,4,0,3,9,2,6
               40 END

    b)   10 DIM N(J)
               20 MAT READ N
               30 MAT PRINT N
               40 DATA 21,31,6,8,42
               50 END

    c)   10 DIM B$(15)
               20 FOR I=1 TO 15
               30 B$(I)=I*2
               40 NEXT I
               50 END

    d)   100 DIM K(15)
              200 FOR A=1 TO 20
              300 K(A)=K(A)+1
              400 NEXT A
              500 MAT PRINT K
              600 END

2.   What printout do the following statements produce?

    a)   10 DIM A(12)
               20 MAT READ A
               30 FOR K=1 TO 12
               40 LET T=T+A(K)
               50 NEXT K
               60 MAT PRINT A;
               70 PRINT T
               80 DATA 6,10,3,8,18,4,9,1,17,7,14,5
               90 END

    b)   10 DIM P(10),C(10)
               20 MAT READ P
               30 MAT READ C
               40 MAT P=P+C
               50 MAT PRINT P;
               60 DATA 100,49,12,26,34,25,11,14,91,3
               70 DATA -40,21,-3,-11,16,46,5,0,17,-3
               80 END

3. Read the following data and store the numbers in a one-dimensional array.

    nnn   DATA 16,49,300,81,147,8,490,1039,67,263

Use an appropriate statement number for your program. Find the total of the numbers and the average value; print all input and computed values.

4. The following is a DATA statement that is to appear in a program.

    nnn   DATA 1,6,2,4,0,8,13,9,7,16,3,14

    a) Treat the values as a one-dimensional array of 12 items. Read the numbers into the table, then INPUT a number and look it up in the table. If that number is found in the table, print THE NUMBER IS IN BUCKET nn. If the number is not in the table, print THE NUMBER IS NOT IN THE TABLE.

    b) Treat the data as a 4 by 3 two-dimensional array. Read the values and proceed as in part a).

5. A firm has sales data for its 12 product lines for the last two years. Each data statement contains the product number, year 1 sales and year 2 sales. They are as follows:

```
nnn   DATA 1625,157,168
nnn   DATA 1813,2450,3116
nnn   DATA 1214,950,1036
nnn   DATA 1398,760,803
nnn   DATA 8274,650,670
nnn   DATA 2100,1047,805
nnn   DATA 7457,3108,3340
nnn   DATA 602,1901,1840
nnn   DATA 3231,65,80
nnn   DATA 5140,530,495
nnn   DATA 3837,16,20
nnn   DATA 6010,2057,2400
```

Note that some products decreased in sales. Read this data into a two-dimensional array and use it to predict year 3 sales. Print the output in the following format:

PRODUCT NUMBER	YEAR 1 SALES	YEAR 2 SALES	PREDICTED YEAR 3 SALES
xxxx	xxxx	xxxx	xxxx
xxxx	xxxx	xxxx	xxxx

6. Use the data from Question 5 to calculate the total sales for each year and the increase or decrease in sales for each product. The total difference should also be calculated. Print the data in the following format:

PRODUCT NUMBER	YEAR 1 SALES	YEAR 2 SALES	DIFFERENCE
xxxx	xxxx	xxxx	xxxx
xxxx	xxxx	xxxx	xxxx
TOTAL	xxxxx	xxxxx	xxxxx

7. Write a program to read DATA statements, each containing a part number and a unit cost. There are 20 parts, and the data are to be stored in arrays.

Now, accept as input from the keyboard a part number and a quantity; find the part number in the array and print the part number, quantity, unit cost and extended cost (quantity * unit cost). If there is no match for the input, print a message to indicate an invalid part number. The last input is part number 9999. Print the total extended cost at the end.

PART NUMBER	QUANTITY	UNIT COST	EXTENDED COST
xxxx	xxx	xx.xx	xxx.xx
xxxx	xxx	xx.xx	xxx.xx
	PLEASE PAY THIS AMOUNT		xxxx.xx

9
Subroutines and Program Organization

Good program organization is indicative of the programmer's ability to clearly define the solution to a programming problem. The use of subroutines can help to achieve a very clear and logical solution to a problem since the "modules" function independently of one another. Thus, an error in one routine is unlikely to adversely affect the performance of the others. This modularity allows easier program modification since additional routines may be added, unnecessary ones deleted or existing routines revised to achieve better performance or different output.

Another advantage of the use of subroutines is that it is necessary to write a given set of instructions only once in a program. The routine can be referenced from any part of the program. Without the availability of subroutines, it would not be unusual, particularly in large programs, to write various sections of logic several times for use in different parts of the program. This leads to wasted storage space and a waste of the programmer's time.

GOSUB AND RETURN STATEMENTS

In BASIC, subroutines are invoked and terminated through the use of the GOSUB and RETURN statements. GOSUB is used to transfer control to a subroutine while RETURN terminates the subroutine and transfers control back to the point immediately following the GOSUB. The general format of the GOSUB and RETURN statements is shown in Figure 9.1.

The following illustration shows the function of the GOSUB and RETURN statements.

```
10   ---
20   ---
30   ---
40   ---
50   GOSUB 120
60   ---
70   ---
80   ---
90   ---
100  ---
110  STOP
120  REM SUBROUTINE BEGINS
130  ---
140  ---
150  RETURN
160  ---
170  ---
```

---

statement number   GOSUB   statement number

statement number   RETURN

FIGURE 9.1   GOSUB and RETURN Statements—General Format

At statement 50, control is transferred to statement 120. Although this is the first statement of the subroutine, there is no special marking of this. Statements 120, 130 and 140 are executed as they would be if encountered in normal program execution. At line 150, the RETURN statement causes a transfer of control back to the point immediately following the original GOSUB, that is, to statement 60.

Example 1:   An Invoice Program

The program in this example reads, calculates and prints. In this respect, it is typical of most programming problems.

DATA statements contain a part number, quantity and cost. The program must calculate the extended cost, add the extended cost to the total and print the part number, quantity, cost and extended cost. The total extended cost is to be printed at the end, which is indicated by a part number of 9999.

The program is organized in such a way that the main logic is a series of GOSUB statements. Each subroutine has a specific purpose, which is shown in a REM statement at the beginning.

The main loop of the program, statements 80 to 140, causes the subroutines to be used in the proper order to read, calculate and print for each data record and to print the total extended cost at the end.

```
00010 REM -- PRINT HEADINGS
00020 PRINT USING 30,
00030:    PART      QUANTITY       UNIT           EXTENDED
00040 PRINT USING 50,
00050:     NUMBER                  COST           COST
00060 LET T=0
00070 REM -- THE MAIN CONTROL LOOP
00080 GOSUB 160
00090 IF I=9999 THEN 130
00100 GOSUB 210
00110 GOSUB 250
00120 GO TO 80
00130 GOSUB 290
00140 STOP
00150 REM -- SUBROUTINE - READS A DATA RECORD
00160 READ I,Q,C
00170 RETURN
00180 REM --
00190 REM -- SUBROUTINE - CALCULATE EXTENDED AND TOTAL COST
00200 REM --
00210 LET E=Q*C
00220 LET T=T+E
```

```
00230 RETURN
00240 REM -- SUBROUTINE - WRITE A DETAIL LINE
00250 PRINT USING 260,I,Q,C,E
00260:    ####        ###        ###.##        ####.##
00270 RETURN
00280 REM -- SUBROUTINE - WRITE THE TOTAL
00290 PRINT
00300 PRINT USING 320,T
00310 PRINT
00320:         TOTAL EXTENDED COST        ####.##
00330 RETURN
00340 DATA 4627,20,1.01
00350 DATA 1752,50,.25
00360 DATA 8563,100,.27
00370 DATA 7452,64,2.74
00380 DATA 8364,24,8.42
00390 DATA 9375,8,.35
00400 DATA 4658,4,5.36
00410 DATA 4645,67,.36
00420 DATA 9999,9,9
00430 END
```

PART NUMBER	QUANTITY	UNIT COST	EXTENDED COST
4627	20	1.01	20.20
1752	50	0.25	12.50
8563	100	0.27	27.00
7452	64	2.74	175.36
8364	24	8.42	202.08
9375	8	0.35	2.80
4658	4	5.36	21.44
4645	67	0.36	24.12

```
TOTAL EXTENDED COST             485.50
```

Example 2:   Adding a Routine

The subroutine facility allows a function to be added very easily without making a great number of changes to existing statements. For instance, in Example 1, data records contain a part number, quantity and cost. The program, as written, reads the data, calculates and prints the line. If the data were required to be in ascending order by part number, the program would require modification. This could be accomplished by adding a GOSUB statement at statement 95 to cause a subroutine to check the sequence of the incoming data. The subroutine is placed at statements 311 to 319, and no alteration is made to any other statement. In case a sequence error occurs, a message is printed, and the program is stopped. Processing continues as long as no error is detected.

The program is listed here twice—the first time with the data arranged in ascending order, the second time with the data in the same sequence as in Example 1. This proves that the subroutine actually performs its required task. If the data are in sequence, the existence of the subroutine is not felt (it is "transparent"); however, when an error is detected, the instructions of the subroutine cause the message to be printed and the program to be interrupted.

```
00010 REM -- PRINT HEADINGS
00020 PRINT USING 30,
00030:     PART       QUANTITY         UNIT          EXTENDED
00040 PRINT USING 50,
00050:   NUMBER                        COST           COST
00060 LET T=0
00070 REM -- THE MAIN CONTROL LOOP
00080 GOSUB 160
00090 IF I=9999 THEN 130
00095 GOSUB 311
00100 GOSUB 190
00110 GOSUB 230
00120 GO TO 80
00130 GOSUB 270
00140 STOP
00150 REM -- SUBROUTINE - READS A DATA RECORD
00160 READ I,Q,C
00170 RETURN
00180 REM -- SUBROUTINE - CALCULATE EXTENDED AND TOTAL COST
00190 LET E=Q*C
00200 LET T=T+E
00210 RETURN
00220 REM -- SUBROUTINE - WRITE A DETAIL LINE
00230 PRINT USING 240,I,Q,C,E
00240:    ####           ###         ###.##         ####.##
00250 RETURN
00260 REM -- SUBROUTINE - WRITE THE TOTAL
00270 PRINT
00280 PRINT USING 300,T
00290 PRINT
00300:           TOTAL EXTENDED COST              ####.##
00310 RETURN
00311 REM -- SUBROUTINE - SEQUENCE CHECK THE DATA
00312 IF I>I1 THEN 318
00313 PRINT "THE LAST PART NUMBER READ IS ";I
00314 PRINT "THIS DATA RECORD IS OUT OF SEQUENCE"
00315 PRINT "PLEASE ENTER THE DATA IN THE PROPER ORDER"
00316 PRINT
00317 STOP
00318 I1=I
00319 RETURN
00320 DATA 1752,50,.25
00330 DATA 4627,20,1.01
00340 DATA 4645,67,.36
00350 DATA 4658,4,5.36
00360 DATA 7452,64,2.74
00370 DATA 8364,24,8.42
00380 DATA 8563,100,.27
00390 DATA 9375,8,.35
00400 DATA 9999,9,9
00410 END
```

PART NUMBER	QUANTITY	UNIT COST	EXTENDED COST
1752	50	0.25	12.50
4627	20	1.01	20.20
4645	67	0.36	24.12
4658	4	5.36	21.44
7452	64	2.74	175.36
8364	24	8.42	202.08
8563	100	0.27	27.00
9375	8	0.35	2.80

TOTAL EXTENDED COST   485.50

```
00010 REM -- PRINT HEADINGS
00020 PRINT USING 30,
00030:     PART        QUANTITY        UNIT        EXTENDED
00040 PRINT USING 50,
00050:     NUMBER                      COST        COST
00060 LET T=0
00070 REM -- THE MAIN CONTROL LOOP
00080 GOSUB 160
00090 IF I=9999 THEN 130
00095 GOSUB 311
00100 GOSUB 190
00110 GOSUB 230
00120 GO TO 80
00130 GOSUB 270
00140 STOP
00150 REM -- SUBROUTINE - READS A DATA RECORD
00160 READ I,Q,C
00170 RETURN
00180 REM -- SUBROUTINE - CALCULATE EXTENDED AND TOTAL COST
00190 LET E=Q*C
00200 LET T=T+E
00210 RETURN
00220 REM -- SUBROUTINE - WRITE A DETAIL LINE
00230 PRINT USING 240,I,Q,C,E
00240:     ####        ###         ###.##        ####.##
00250 RETURN
00260 REM -- SUBROUTINE - WRITE THE TOTAL
00270 PRINT
00280 PRINT USING 300,T
00290 PRINT
00300:          TOTAL EXTENDED COST            ####.##
00310 RETURN
00311 REM -- SUBROUTINE - SEQUENCE CHECK THE DATA
00312 IF I>I1 THEN 318
00313 PRINT "THE LAST PART NUMBER READ IS ";I
00314 PRINT "THIS DATA RECORD IS OUT OF SEQUENCE"
00315 PRINT "PLEASE ENTER THE DATA IN THE PROPER ORDER"
00316 PRINT
00317 STOP
00318 I1=I
00319 RETURN
00320 DATA 4627,20,1.01
00330 DATA 1752,50,.25
00340 DATA 8563,100,.27
00350 DATA 7452,64,2.74
00360 DATA 8364,24,8.42
00370 DATA 9375,8,.35
00380 DATA 4658,4,5.36
00390 DATA 4645,67,.36
00400 DATA 9999,9,9
00410 END
```

```
     PART        QUANTITY        UNIT        EXTENDED
     NUMBER                      COST        COST
     4627        20              1.01        20.20
THE LAST PART NUMBER READ IS  1752
THIS DATA RECORD IS OUT OF SEQUENCE
PLEASE ENTER THE DATA IN THE PROPER ORDER
```

MULTIPLE USES OF ONE SUBROUTINE

A subroutine may also be called from many places within the program; thus, there may be several GOSUB's referring to the same statement number and indicating that the logic of the subroutine is to be executed at various points in the program and not just at one particular location. As each GOSUB is encountered, control branches to the subroutine, it is executed, and control then returns to the statement following the GOSUB.

The following statements show how a subroutine may be referenced more than once in a program.

```
100   GOSUB 300
105
      ---
      ---
150   GOSUB 300
160
      ---
      ---
      ---
      ---
300   LET N=N-1
310   LET J3=N**2
320   RETURN
      ---
      ---
      ---
      ---
```

In this illustration, as the program executes statement 100, control branches to statement 300. At this point, statements 300 through 320 are executed. When the RETURN statement at line 320 is reached, control branches back to statement 105. The program continues to execute sequentially until statement 150 is reached, at which time control again goes to subroutine 300. This time when the RETURN statement is executed, control branches back to statement 160. Thus, the point to which control returns is dependent on the location of the GOSUB that invoked the subroutine.

NESTED SUBROUTINES

The following statements show the use of nested subroutines.

```
100   GOSUB 200
110
      ---
      ---
      ---
```

```
200   LET A(J)=K(N,3)
210   GOSUB 300
220
---
240   RETURN
---
---
---
---
---
300   PRINT A(J)
310   RETURN
```

In this illustration, when statement 100 is reached, control branches to subroutine 200, and the first statement is executed. At statement 210, control branches to subroutine 300. When the RETURN in this subroutine is reached at statement 310, control branches back to statement 200, and execution continues in subroutine 200. When the RETURN in statement 240 is reached, control finally branches back to statement 110. Thus, at one point in time, subroutine 200 had been invoked, but subroutine 300 is also invoked once statement 210 has been reached; in a sense, they are both in control of the program since subroutine 200 requires the use of subroutine 300 for its successful execution.

Example 3:   Monthly Sales Commission Program

Here is a more complex example that could require repetition of many lines of coding if the GOSUB were not used. The sales representatives of a company are paid a commission on monthly sales according to the following table.

Sales	Commission
up to $500.00	3%
$500.01 — $1000.00	7%
$1000.01 — $2500.00	12%
over $2500.00	16%

Each sale is recorded on a data record containing the sales representative's identification number and the amount sold.

A report is required to print one line for each sales representative showing the identification number, the amount sold by that representative and the commission to be paid. The grand total sales and grand total commission are required at the end of the report. Since all records for one individual must be together, the records must be in sequence by identification number.

The signal to calculate the commission and to print the line is a new identification number. This, however, poses a problem at the end, when the 9999 indicates the end of data. In this case, the commission for the final sales representative must be calculated and printed before the final totals are printed.

The heading is repeated after every five lines of output. Notice how the spacing of lines is accomplished.

```
00010 LET L=5
00020 GOSUB 460
00030 REM - MAIN LOOP
00040 READ I,A
00050 IF I=9999 THEN 200
00060 REM - IS THIS THE FIRST TIME?
00070 IF P=0 THEN 160
00080 REM - IS THE DATA IN THE PROPER ORDER?
00090 IF I<P THEN 270
00100 REM - IS THIS A DIFFERENT SALESMAN?
00110 IF I<>P THEN 130
00120 GO TO 170
00130 GOSUB 300
00140 GOSUB 420
00150 GOSUB 460
00160 LET P=I
00170 LET T=T+A
00180 GO TO 40
00190 REM - END OF PROGRAM ROUTINE
00200 GOSUB 300
00210 GOSUB 420
00220 GOSUB 460
00230 GOSUB 640
00240 PRINT "END OF PROGRAM"
00250 GO TO 1200
00260 REM - SEQUENCE ERROR
00270 PRINT "THIS RECORD IS OUT OF SEQUENCE",I;A
00280 STOP
00290 REM - CALCULATE SALESMAN'S COMMISSION
00300 IF T>2500 THEN 390
00310 IF T>1000 THEN 370
00320 IF T>500 THEN 350
00330 LET C=T*.03
00340 GO TO 400
00350 LET C=T*.07
00360 GO TO 400
00370 LET C=T*.12
00380 GO TO 400
00390 LET C=T*.16
00400 RETURN
00410 REM - ACCUMULATE GRAND TOTALS
00420 LET T1=T1+T
00430 LET C1=C1+C
00440 RETURN
00450 REM - PRINT ROUTINE - HEADINGS EVERY 5TH LINE
00460 IF L<5 THEN 570
00470 REM - SPACE 3 LINES
00480 GOSUB 710
00490 PRINT USING 500,
00500:      SALES          SALE          COMMISSION
00510 PRINT USING 520,
00520:      REPRESENTATIVE     AMOUNT
00530 LET L=0
```

```
00540 REM - SPACE 1 LINE
00550 GOSUB 730
00560 IF P=0 THEN 610
00570 PRINT USING 580,P,T,C
00580:        ####           ####.##              ####.##
00590 LET L=L+1
00600 LET T=0
00610 RETURN
00620 REM - PRINT FINAL TOTALS
00630 REM - SPACE 3 LINES
00640 GOSUB 710
00650 PRINT USING 660,
00660:                    ========             ========
00670 PRINT USING 680,T1,C1
00680:    GRAND TOTALS    #####.##          #####.##
00690 REM - SPACING FOR LISTING
00700 PRINT
00710 PRINT
00720 PRINT
00730 PRINT
00740 RETURN
00750 DATA 2120,345.50
00760 DATA 2120,560.25
00770 DATA 2305,556.86
00780 DATA 2305,225.35
00790 DATA 2305,99.30
00800 DATA 2362,564.87
00810 DATA 2362,50.60
00820 DATA 2362,1025.45
00830 DATA 2362,827.56
00840 DATA 2362,934.46
00850 DATA 2362,96.58
00860 DATA 2362,315.37
00870 DATA 2362,65.69
00880 DATA 2708,739.72
00890 DATA 3421,12.43
00900 DATA 3421,1793.71
00910 DATA 4007,294.75
00920 DATA 4007,805.32
00930 DATA 4007,1395.73
00940 DATA 4158,1483.61
00950 DATA 4385,65.78
00960 DATA 4385,824.98
00970 DATA 4385,475.22
00980 DATA 4385,108.38
00990 DATA 4770,453.68
01000 DATA 4770,2957.56
01010 DATA 5391,693.68
01020 DATA 5575,952.76
01030 DATA 5575,35.68
01040 DATA 5575,67.21
01050 DATA 6040,1192.46
01060 DATA 6258,54.62
01070 DATA 6258,443.45
01080 DATA 6258,552.76
01090 DATA 6705,453.66
01100 DATA 6860,1396.64
01110 DATA 6860,1210.73
01120 DATA 6860,179.68
01130 DATA 7038,1793.62
01140 DATA 7038,2010.69
01150 DATA 7277,607.34
01160 DATA 7277,463.83
01170 DATA 7277,92.46
01180 DATA 8105,1752.56
01190 DATA 9999,9
01200 END
```

SALES REPRESENTATIVE	SALE AMOUNT	COMMISSION
2120	905.75	63.40
2305	881.51	61.71
2362	3880.58	620.89
2708	739.72	51.78
3421	1806.14	216.74

SALES REPRESENTATIVE	SALE AMOUNT	COMMISSION
4007	2495.80	299.50
4158	1483.61	178.03
4385	1474.36	176.92
4770	3411.24	545.80
5391	693.68	48.56

SALES REPRESENTATIVE	SALE AMOUNT	COMMISSION
5575	1055.65	126.68
6040	1192.46	143.10
6258	1050.83	126.10
6705	453.66	13.61
6860	2787.05	445.93

SALES REPRESENTATIVE	SALE AMOUNT	COMMISSION
7038	3804.31	608.69
7277	1163.63	139.64
8105	1752.56	210.31

	========	========
GRAND TOTALS	31032.54	4077.37

END OF PROGRAM

COMMON ERRORS

1.   50   GO TO 150

        ---
        150   READ A,B,C
        160   RETURN

No return is possible unless the subroutine has been invoked by a GOSUB statement. *Correction:* 50   GOSUB 150

2.   100   GOSUB 400

          ---

    400   PRINT A,B

          ---

    600   END

There is no RETURN statement to cause control to transfer back to the statement following the GOSUB statement. *Correction:* Place the RETURN statement at the proper point.

3.   80   GOSUB 90
    90   READ N,M

          ---

    200   RETURN

The main program and the subroutine are not separated. When the RETURN is executed, control passes to the statement following the GOSUB. In this case, that statement is part of the subroutine. This could cause a loop or other logic problems. *Correction:* Place a STOP or GO TO statement at statement number 85, depending on the problem.

4.   40   IF A=10 THEN 240
    50   K=K+1

          ---

    240   READ X,Y

          ---

    270   RETURN

Control is passed to the subroutine by the IF statement. No return is possible unless a GOSUB statement is used.
Correction: 40   IF A <> 10 THEN 50
              45   GOSUB 250
              50   K = K + 1
                   ---

5.   75   GOSUB 300

          ---

    120   PRINT X,N

    300

```
      ---
350   GO TO 120
      ---
400   RETURN
```

Statement 75 indicates that a subroutine begins at statement 300 and passes control to there. Part way through the subroutine, control is passed to statement number 120 by a GO TO statement; this makes the GOSUB statement ineffective. *Correction:* The logic to branch to a specific statement should be handled in the main section.

QUESTIONS

1. In what respect is a GOSUB like a GO TO statement? How do they differ?

2. Write a subroutine, starting with line 180, that reads three values, N, A and R. If the value of N is less than the previous value of N (N1), write the message SEQUENCE ERROR and stop the program. Otherwise, move N to N1 and go back to the main section of the program.

3. What values are printed by the following programs?

a)
```
10   A=5
20   B=3
30   C=12
40   GOSUB 200
50   GOSUB 300
60   GOSUB 400
70   STOP
200  IF A+B>C THEN 220
210  C=C+2
220  RETURN
300  IF C<A*B THEN 320
310  A=A+2
320  B=B+1
330  RETURN
400  PRINT A
410  PRINT B
420  PRINT C
430  RETURN
440  END
```

b)
```
10   GOSUB 100
20   GOSUB 110
30   GOSUB 120
40   STOP
100  K=40
105  RETURN
110  J=(K/10)*(K/20)
115  RETURN
120  L=L+1
130  GOSUB 200
140  RETURN
200  PRINT J,K,L
210  RETURN
220  END
```

4. Identify the errors in the following programs.

a)
```
80   READ A
90   GOSUB 200
100  PRINT A
110  GO TO 90
200  LET A=A*4
210  END
```

b)
```
10   LET M=470
20   LET N=30
30   GO TO 100
40   READ S
50   PRINT P,S
60   STOP
100  LET P=M-N
110  RETURN
120  END
```

c)
```
10   READ J
20   GOSUB 50
30   PRINT A,J
40   IF A < 10 THEN 10
50   LET A=A+1
60   RETURN
70   END
```

5. Read data records containing:

Vendor Number	6 Digits
Item Number	7 Digits
Description	20 Characters maximum
Unit Cost	7 Digits (2 decimal)
Quantity	5 Digits

Produce a vendor report showing the input data as well as a computed total cost per record. Allow a discount rate of 1% per $1000 to a maximum of 5% for $5000.00 or over. Sequence check records on item number within vendor number. There may be any number of records per vendor. Allow for a maximum of thirty lines under each heading. If this is exceeded, print new headings after leaving appropriate spacing.

6. Write a program for a college controller to compute for one semester:

a) the tuition due from each student;

b) the total tuition from all students;

c)   the average tuition per student;

d)   the average number of credits per student; and

e)   the student with the highest number of credits.

Tuition due is calculated on this basis:

    (i)   if a student enrolls for ten credits or less, he pays tuition at the rate of $80 per credit; and

    (ii)   if a student enrolls for more than ten credits, he pays a tuition of $800.

The input contains one card for each subject for which a student enrolls. The cards are sorted by student number. The number of cards for each student is not constant, that is, there may be one card for one student, six cards for the next and so on. The card format is: student number, subject number and number of credits (maximum—2).

The output should consist of one line per student, showing student number, number of subjects, number of credits and tuition. The total should appear at the end of the listing.

10
Files

The use of files in BASIC allows the programmer to store data on tape or disk files that are external to the program. In addition to eliminating or reducing the need for data statements, files permit storing data for access by any other BASIC program. This is not the case with the DATA statement, which may only be accessed by the program containing it.

Files may be stored and accessed in several different formats, depending on the level of BASIC supplied by a specific computer. Sequential access is generally available in all systems and is the method discussed in this chapter. Other access methods include direct access, where records are identified by a key and may be read selectively by supplying the key of the record required, and indexed sequential where records are stored sequentially but use an index that specifies the location of the record on the file for direct accessing.

SEQUENTIAL TAPE AND DISK FILES

Sequential files may be thought of as DATA statements that reside on a magentic tape or disk. Data from these files are read sequentially, starting at the beginning of the file and progressing through each item of data until the end of the file is reached. Figure 10.1 shows how data might appear on magnetic tape. The major differences between files and DATA statements are the lack of a statement number and the missing keyword DATA. In other words, just the data are present on the file.

A significant characteristic of tape is its ability to access data sequentially but not directly. This is also true of sequential disk files, but disk may use other access methods. Figure 10.2 shows data stored sequentially on a disk storage device, which may be either a floppy disk or a hard disk. Although storage methods may differ slightly from one type of disk to another, this is not usually apparent to the programmer; therefore, we will limit ourselves to general concepts here.

As with tape, disk stores only the data. In this case, the data are stored sequentially around the tracks, which are defined magnetically on the disk surface. The number of bytes (characters) that can

RECORD 1	RECORD 2
110,"J.C. JACKSON",3,25,1965	

FIGURE 10.1 A Sequential Tape File

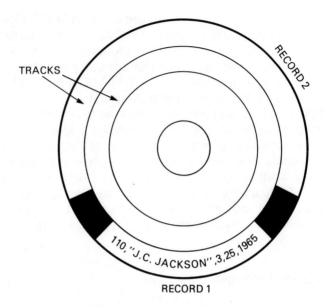

FIGURE 10.2 A Sequential Disk File

be stored on each track and the number of tracks on a surface vary considerably from one disk to another.

OPEN AND CLOSE STATEMENTS

The OPEN statement, is used to indicate that an external file is to be used in a BASIC program. When more than one file is used, a separate OPEN statement is included in the program for each file. As we can see from the general format (Figure 10.3), several parameters are used to describe the file and to define how it is to be used. Unfortunately, there is no standard for this statement, and its format may be quite different on other systems. However, the essential reason for its use remains the same.

The filename is a name by which we may choose to identify our file on the disk or tape. It is similar to a name we might choose to

statement number OPEN filename FOR $\begin{Bmatrix} \text{INPUT} \\ \text{OUTPUT} \end{Bmatrix}$ AS FILE# n

,ACCESS $\begin{Bmatrix} \text{READ} \\ \text{WRITE} \end{Bmatrix}$

FIGURE 10.3 OPEN Statement—General Format

identify a program when we save it on the computer. The attributes INPUT and OUTPUT define whether a file is to be created (OUTPUT) or an existing file is to be read (INPUT). FILE# n defines a number that will be used to identify the file in the current program. Other programs may use a different file number but must use the same filename. Some systems use the file number to identify the device, such as a cassette tape, rather than the file. The last attribute that we must select is either READ or WRITE. A file that we want to READ is accessed with the INPUT# statement in the program. When we want to WRITE on a file, the PRINT# statement is used. These are discussed later in this chapter.

Suppose that a new file of payroll records is to be created from a program. The OPEN statement might look like this:

30   OPEN PAYROLL FOR OUTPUT AS FILE# 1,ACCESS WRITE

This means that the file is identified as PAYROLL on disk. This program references this file as file 1, and a PRINT# statement is used to WRITE on the file. Another program may read this file after it is created. This second program could use the following OPEN statement.

20   OPEN PAYROLL FOR INPUT AS FILE# 3,ACCESS READ

The file must still be identified as PAYROLL in order for the system to find it on disk. However, it may use a different file number in this program; of course, number 1 could be used if no other file was referenced by this number.

---

statement number   CLOSE# n

FIGURE 10.4   CLOSE Statement—General Format

Figure 10.4 gives the general format for the CLOSE statement. This statement is used when we are finished processing the data from a file. This often occurs at the end of the program, but it may be used anytime after we are finished with the file. A CLOSE statement for the PAYROLL file that was to be created is:

900   CLOSE# 1

The second use of the PAYROLL file would be closed as follows:

80   CLOSE# 3

Some BASIC interpreters permit several files to be closed at the same time. An example is:

250 CLOSE# 1,2,5

PRINT # STATEMENT

Writing data on a file uses a special form of the PRINT statement (Figure 10.5). This works like an output to the printer or screen except that the output is on a magnetic device.

---
statement number   PRINT# n, variables

FIGURE 10.5 PRINT# Statement—General Format

The parameter n refers to the file number specified in the OPEN statement. For instance, the PAYROLL file discussed earlier could have a number written on it with the statement:

60 PRINT# 1,E

where E represents an Employee Number and the 1 refers to the file number in the OPEN statement. A name could be written on the same file with the statement:

70 PRINT# 1,N$

The variable N$ refers to the alphanumeric variable for the name.

A file often requires a list of data, which represents a record for a specific transaction. For instance, the PAYROLL file might require an Employee Number, Name, Rate and Department. Of course, a real payroll problem would require far more data than this. When these data are to be written on the file, it is necessary to have characters to separate each field so that the system will know when one field ends and the next one begins. These are called field separator characters, and commas are usually used for this purpose.

To write the above four fields on disk, we could use the following statement:

50 PRINT# 1,E;",";N$;",";R;",";D

In this example, the fields are separated by commas on the file. The semicolons are used in the PRINT format so that the data are compacted. Otherwise, each field would occupy a separate print region as it does on printed output; this unnecessarily wastes space on the disk or tape. Data on the file are stored as:

250, "J.D. DOE",7.50, 30

indicating Employee Number 250, Name of J.D. DOE, Rate of 7.50 and Department 30. Notice that no identification of the fields appear on the file. The programmer must know what fields are on the file and reference them accordingly.

CREATING A DATA FILE

The following is a program that creates a file of personnel information. The file is given the name PERSON and is referenced in this program as file number 1. Data for the program are supplied in DATA statements althought they could have been supplied during execution with an INPUT statement. The fields are Employee Number (E), Name (N$), Job Category (J), Department (D) and Year Employed (Y). The disk file is opened in statement 10. Statement 20 reads these data, and line 30 looks for an Employee Number 999 to indicate the end of the file. Statement 50 writes the five data fields on the disk file with comma separators. When all the records except the 9's have been written on the disk, statement 70 closes the file.

```
00010 OPEN "PERSON" FOR OUTPUT AS FILE #1, ACCESS WRITE
00020 READ E,N$,J,D,Y
00030 IF E=999 THEN 70
00050 PRINT #1,E;",";N$;",";J;",";D;",";Y
00060 GO TO 20
00070 CLOSE #1
00080 DATA 110,"J.C. JACKSON",3,25,1965
00090 DATA 115,"A.F. KENWOOD",2,30,1975
00100 DATA 121,"H.H. BENSON",1,25,1977
00110 DATA 143,"C.Z. DAWSON",4,40,1968
00120 DATA 999," ",9,9,9
00130 END
```

INPUT# STATEMENT

Once a file has been created, it may be accessed by any BASIC program. Figure 10.6 shows the general format of the INPUT# statement used for reading data from an existing file. The

---

statement number   INPUT# n, variables

FIGURE 10.6   INPUT# Statement—General Format

operation of INPUT# is similar to the INPUT statement. A list of one or more variables, which corresponds to the data coming from the file, is given. Data from the file are assigned field by field to the variables in the order listed. Unlike the INPUT statement, the IN-PUT# statement does not wait for an operator to enter data but continues processing without noticeable delay.

A statement to read a quantity from file 3 is:

70   INPUT# 3,Q

A file containing Part Number(P), Quantity(Q) and Description(D$) could be read as follows:

110   INPUT# 2,P,Q,D$

IFEND# AND IFMORE# STATEMENTS

When a file is being read, it is necessary to know when all of the data have been processed. If DATA statements are supplying the data, an end-of-file record containing 9's is usually supplied. This is detected by the program, and control branches to the end-of-file routine. This same method could be used with files; however, a superior method that does not require a special end-of-file record is available. Rather the computer senses when the end of the file has been reached and advises the program by means of a special status indicator. This indicator may be tested by the IFEND# and IF-MORE# statements shown in Figure 10.7.

The IFEND# statement tests the status of the file number specified. If the end of that file has been reached, the program branches to the statement coded in the THEN or GOTO. If the end of the file has not been reached, the program continues at the next consecutive statement. For example:

```
10   IFEND# 1 THEN 200
20   INPUT# 1,N$,A$,P
30
---
---
190   GOTO 10
200
```

This program reads and processes data from file 1. Each time that statement 190 is reached, control passes back to statement 10,

statement number IFEND# n $\begin{Bmatrix} \text{THEN} \\ \text{GOTO} \end{Bmatrix}$ statement number

statement number IFMORE# n $\begin{Bmatrix} \text{THEN} \\ \text{GOTO} \end{Bmatrix}$ statement number

FIGURE 10.7   IFEND# and IFMORE# Statements—General Formats

which is the IFEND# instruction. Here the status is tested to verify for end-of-file status. If the end has not been reached, the program continues with statement 20, and the next set of data is read. Eventually, the end of the file is reached, and the program passes from statement 10 to statement 200. Here the program can print totals, do other processing or simply close the file(s) and terminate.

The IFMORE# statement performs the same function as the IFEND# statement except that it asks if there is more data to be read. Here is an example:

```
20   INPUT# 1,N$,A$,P
30
     ---
     ---
190  IFMORE# 1 GOTO 20
200
```

This program continues down to line 190, where the IFMORE# statement is located. If there is more data to be read from the file at this point, the program will GOTO statement 20. After this has happened a number of times, depending on the amount of data in the file, there will not be anymore data in file 1. When statement 190 is reached this time, the GOTO statement will not be executed, and the program will continue at statement 200.

READING A DATA FILE

We are now ready to read a file containing Employee Number (E), Name (N$), Job Category (J), Department (D) and Year Employed (E). The program reads the five data items for each employee and prints them. When the end of the file is reached, determined by the IFEND# statement in line 30, the file is closed in statement 90, and the program is terminated. Notice that, after each record is processed, the program branches back to the IFEND# statement, which must be tested each time before another attempt is made to read

```
00010 REM READ AND PRINT DISK FILE
00020 OPEN "PERSON..1" FOR INPUT AS FILE#1, ACCESS READ
00030 IFEND #1 THEN 90
00040 REM E=EMPLOYEE NUMBER N$=NAME J= JOB CATEGORY
00050 REM D=DEPARTMENT Y=YEAR EMPLOYED
00060 INPUT #1,E,N$,J,D,Y
00070 PRINT E,N$,J,D,Y
00080 GOTO 30
00090 CLOSE #1
00100 END

110        J.C. JACKSON    3       25      1965
115        A.F. KENWOOD    2       30      1975
121        H.H. BENSON     1       25      1977
143        C.Z. DAWSON     4       40      1968
```

data. Also notice that the OPEN statement is encountered only once at the beginning of the program; control never branches back here otherwise an error occurs.

Once a data file is created, many types of processing may be done with it. This depends on the data available in the file and the needs of the users of the data. The last program was quite simple, but let us take the same file and do some other types of processing against it. To do this, it will be necessary to read the file more than once. This may be accomplished by the RESTORE# statement. It has a quite simple format:

70   RESTORE# 1

It functions in the same way as the RESTORE statement for READ and DATA statements. In this case, the RESTORE# statement sets us to the beginning of file 1, which permits the program to read all of the data from this file again.

Two reports are required from this program. The first is a listing of and the total number of employees hired before 1970. When this list is completed, a second list is required of the number of employees in Department 25 who are trainees. Trainees are identified by a Job Category code of 1. Figure 10.8 shows the solution to this problem.

Statements 10 to 140 find and print the employees hired before 1970. This section of the program uses the IFEND# statement to recognize the end of the file. Each record read in statement 60 is tested for the appropriate year in statement 70. Data with a year before 1970 are printed in statement 90, and 1 is added to N in line 100 to count the number of employees who satisfy the criteria. When all the records have been processed, the program branches to statement 120, and the total is printed.

The second half of the program is between statements 150 and 270. The file is restored in statement 170, and each record is read for the second time at statement 180. This time, the data are checked for Department 25; this check is followed by a test for a Job Category of 1. If either of these tests fails, the program goes to line 230, the IFMORE statement, to see whether there is anymore data to be read. If so, the program goes back to statement 180 and reads the next record. If the conditions tested were satisfied, then statement 210 counts the record, and line 220 prints the Employee Number and Name from the file. The program then tests for more data. When all data have been read, the total is printed in line 250, and statement 260 closes the file.

```
00010 OPEN "PERSON..1" FOR INPUT AS FILE#1,ACCESS READ
00020 REM FIND EMPLOYEES HIRED BEFORE 1970
00030 IFEND #1 THEN 120
00040 REM E = EMPLOYEE NUMBER N$ = NAME
00050 REM J = JOB CATEGORY D = DEPT Y = YEAR EMPLOYED
00060 INPUT #1,E,N$,J,D,Y
00070 IF Y<1970 THEN 90
00080 GOTO 30
00090 PRINT E,N$,J,D,Y
00100 N=N+1
00110 GOTO 30
00120 PRINT
00130 PRINT "THERE ARE ";N;" PERSONS EMPLOYED BEFORE 1970"
00140 PRINT
00150 N=0
00160 REM FIND EMPLOYEES IN DEPT 25, JOB 1
00170 RESTORE #1
00180 INPUT#1,E,N$,J,D,Y
00190 IF D<>25 THEN 230
00200 IF J<>1 THEN 230
00210 N=N+1
00220 PRINT E,N$
00230 IFMORE #1 THEN 180
00240 PRINT
00250 PRINT N;" EMPLOYEES ARE IN DEPT 25 WITH JOB CATEGORY 1"
00260 CLOSE #1
00270 END

READY
RUNNH
 110        J.C. JACKSON    3        25        1965
 143        C.Z. DAWSON     4        40        1968

THERE ARE  2  PERSONS EMPLOYED BEFORE 1970

 121        H.H. BENSON

 1  EMPLOYEES ARE IN DEPT 25 WITH JOB CATEGORY 1
```

FIGURE 10.8   Reading a File Twice

UPDATING A DATA FILE

A very common programming application in business is the updating of master files. This involves processing a series of transactions against a master file and in turn creating a new master, which contains revisions of existing records, additions of new records, deletions of obsolete records and records from the master that did not require updating. These are the primary goals of a file update program, and, no matter how complex a file update program may become, the logic basically revolves around these goals.

For this application, we will use a master file that represents a number of subscribers to a magazine. Updates are processed against the records of these subscribers to provide an updated master that can show new customers, renewal of subscriptions or deletion of old customers.

The system flowchart for this program is shown in Figure 10.9.

The purpose of this system flowchart is to show the various input and output files of the program. In this system, there is a subscription master file (MASTER) and an updated subscription master file (UPDATED). All subscriptions presently in the system are on MASTER. Transactions are brought in from transaction data records. This is shown as paper tape in the diagram, but in our program these will be data records that are included in the program itself.

These transactions are processed against the subscription master file, and the various types of updating are done. As this updating occurs, records are written on the new master file. UPDATED then contains the most up-to-date version of the customer subscriptions. Errors that may occur during the run are printed on the Error Report.

The transactions can be of three different types, and these types are identified by a code, which is the second element in the transaction data record. This one-digit code identifies the type of

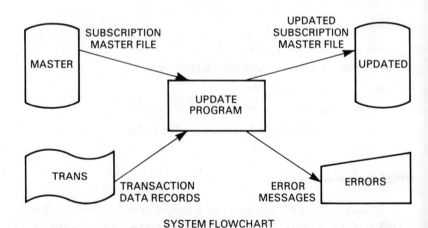

SYSTEM FLOWCHART

FIGURE 10.9 Subscription File Update

transaction and indicates the kind of updating that is to be done by the program.

The three codes are:

Code	Update Type
1	Change of Address.
2	New Customer when there is no equal master or renewal for a year (52 weeks) on an equal master.
3	Deletion if the number of weeks remaining is zero.

The code 1 transaction is used to change the address of an existing customer. This requires that an equal customer number be found on the master file. When this is found, the address from the data record is moved to the address in the master record.

Code 2 can involve two different types of updating. If no equal master record is found for code 2, this implies that a new customer record is to be created on the updated master file. However, if there already is an existing customer on the master file, a check is made to see that the name on the master is the same as the customer's name on the transaction. If so, this confirms that it is a valid code 2, and a renewal for one year is made on the master file.

Code 3 deletes an obsolete customer. To check for the validity of the deletion, the program ensures that the number of weeks remaining on the subscription is at zero. If the number of weeks has not reached zero, there is still time left on the customer's subscription, and the deletion transaction is considered to be an error.

Figures 10.10 and 10.11 show the program flowchart for the subscription update. The first of these is the mainline program flowchart, which deals with the mainline logic. The second deals with the subroutine for reading a master record and a subroutine for reading a transaction record.

The mainline flowchart begins by reading a record from each of the master and the transaction files. The customer number in each of these files is compared to see what relationship exists between the master and the transaction. If the numbers are equal, then codes 1, 2 or 3 are permitted. If it is a code 1, a change is made to that master record, and the program branches back to get another transaction. Notice that at this time another master is not read, and neither is the updated master written. The reason for this is that it is possible that there are more than one update per master record. Thus, by holding the master record temporarily in the program, we are able to apply any number of updates to it.

If there is code 2 and the customer numbers are equal, then a check is made to see whether the names on the records are also

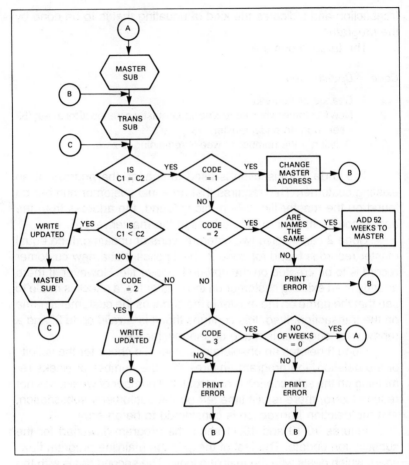

FIGURE 10.10 Mainline Program Flowchart

equal; if they are, 52 is added to the number of weeks remaining in the master record. However, if the names are different, then an error message is printed.

On a code 3, a check is made to see whether the number of weeks remaining in the master is equal to zero; if it does, then the program branches back to read another master. This effectively deletes the existing master since a copy of it has not been written on the updated master file.

If the customer number in the master is less than the customer number in the transaction, this indicates that there is no updating at this time for this master record. This could mean that there had never been any updating for it or that we have processed all of the updating

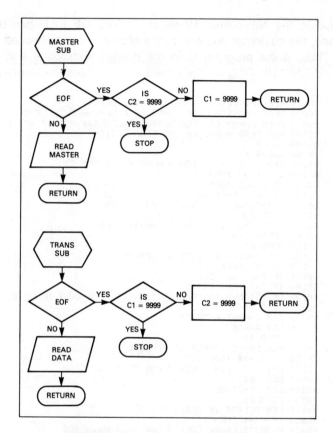

FIGURE 10.11   Subroutine Flowchart

and have now read a new customer number from the transaction file. In either case, we wish to have a copy of this record on the new master, and the command to write UPDATED is given. Since the new master has been written, we need an input master record for processing; thus, a command is given to read from the master file. At this point, we go back to compare the customer numbers.

Finally, if the customer number on the master is greater than the customer number on the transaction, there is only one possibility: a transaction code of two. If it is a code 2, the data from a transaction is written on UPDATED and we go back to read another transaction. This has created a new master record on the updated master file.

The subroutines for reading the master and transaction are similar. In either case, when the subroutine is entered, a check is first made to see whether the END OF FILE has been reached on that file. If not, then a record is read, and the program returns to the point that called the subroutine. However, if END OF FILE has been reached, the customer number on the alternate file is checked. Thus, if the program is in the master subroutine and has reached END OF FILE on the master, it compares the transaction

```
00010 REM SUBSCRIPTION MASTER FILE UPDATE
00020 OPEN "MASTER" FOR INPUT AS FILE#1,ACCESS READ
00030 OPEN "UPDATED" FOR OUTPUT AS FILE#2,ACCESS WRITE
00040 REM READ A MASTER AND TRANSACTION
00050 GOSUB 360
00060 GOSUB 440
00070 REM COMPARE CUSTOMER NUMBERS C1 AND C2
00080 IF C1=C2 THEN 170
00090 IF C1<C2 THEN 130
00100 IF C<>2 THEN 200
00110 PRINT#2,C2;","!52;","!M$;","!B$
00120 GOTO 60
00130 PRINT #2,C1;","!W1;","!N$;","!A$
00140 GOSUB 360
00150 GOTO 80
00160 REM CHECK FOR TYPE OF UPDATE
00170 IF C=1 THEN 230
00180 IF C=2 THEN 260
00190 IF C=3 THEN 320
00200 PRINT"INVALID TRANSACTION CODE FOR CUST NO. ";C2
00210 GOTO 60
00220 REM CHANGE ADDRESS
00230 LET A$=B$
00240 GOTO 60
00250 REM NEW CUSTOMER OR RENEWAL
00260 IF N$=M$ THEN 290
00270 PRINT"ILLEGAL CODE 2 FOR CUST NO. ";C2
00280 GOTO 60
00290 LET W1=W1+52
00300 GOTO 60
00310 REM DELETE IF WEEKS = 0
00320 IF W1=0 THEN 50
00330 PRINT"ILLEGAL CODE 3 FOR CUST NO. ";C2
00340 GOTO 60
00350 REM READ MASTER FILE
00360 IFEND#1 THEN 390
00370 INPUT #1,C1,W1,N$,A$
00380 RETURN
00390 IF C2=9999 THEN 420
00400 LET C1=9999
00410 RETURN
00420 STOP
00430 REM READ TRANSACTIONS
00440 IF C2=9999 THEN 470
00450 READ C2,C,M$,B$
00460 RETURN
00470 IF C1=9999 THEN 500
00480 LET C2=9999
00490 RETURN
00500 STOP
00510 DATA 1010,1,"H SOLLENS","17 BRADLEY"
00520 DATA 1040,1,"E BELZIL","6 LEGGET DR"
00530 DATA 1101,2,"E BELZIL","6 LEGGETT DR"
00540 DATA 1101,3,"D SMITH","54 RUSCIA BLVD"
00550 DATA 1350,2,"W O'HARA","568  PERTH"
00560 DATA 1400,2,"J JONES","15 PEARL DR"
00570 DATA 9999,1,"A","1"
```

FIGURE 10.12 Subscription File Update Program

customer number to see if it is equal to 9's. If it is, this indicates that the END OF FILE had been previously reached on the transaction file; thus, the program has reached END OF FILE on both input files, and there is nothing left to do, so it stops. However, if the transaction file's customer number does not contain 9's, this indicates that there are still transactions to be processed. In this case, 9's are assigned to the master's customer number, and the program returns to the mainline logic.

The effect of assigning 9's to the master customer number C1 is that a comparison of C1 greater than C2 is always obtained. This indicates that only new customers may be added to the file at this point. This makes sense because, if there are no master records remaining, they cannot be updated.

Similarly, in the transaction subroutine, the same kinds of checks are made. If END OF FILE has been reached in the transaction, then the master customer number is compared to see whether it is equal to 9's; if it is, then the program is terminated. If it is not equal to 9's, it indicates that there are still master records to be read, in which case the transaction customer number C2 is set to 9's. The effect of this is that C1 is less than C2; if we look back in the mainline flowchart, we see that, under this condition, each remaining master record is written out on the new master. This condition indicates that the remaining master records have no update transactions to be applied to them. In this case, we only wish to write them out on the new master as they appear on the input; therefore, we write the record, read a new master record and continue the process until

```
01010 , 10 , H SOLLENS , 12 BRISTOL AVE
01025 , 52 , J DOWNINGS , 1 DEAUVILLE
01030 , 128 , K JOHNSON , 55 OAKMOUNT
01078 , 1 , E SCOTT , 30 LOMAR
01101 , 0 , D SMITH , 54 RUSCIA BLVD
01350 , 28 , W O'HARA , 568 PERTH
```
Subscription Master File

```
INVALID TRANSACTION CODE FOR CUST NO.  1040
ILLEGAL CODE 2 FOR CUST NO.  1101
```
Error Messages

```
1010   10    H SOLLENS    17 BRADLEY
1025   52    J DOWNING    1 DEAUVILLE
1030   128   K JOHNSON    55 OAKMOUNT
1078   1     E SCOTT      30 LOMAR
1350   80    W O'HARA     568 PERTH
1400   52    J JONES      15 PEARL DR
```
Updated Subscription File

FIGURE 10.13   Results of Processing

END OF FILE is reached on the master file.

The BASIC program for the subscription file update is shown in Figure 10.12. Essentially, the logic discussed for the flowchart is followed in this program.

Figure 10.13 shows the results from a run of this program. The first part is the master file used for the test run of the program. Following this is a list of error messages generated as a result of processing the transactions in the program. The final section is a copy of the updated master showing the results of the update program.

QUESTIONS

1. File PROD contains records of products and the costs that relate to each product. Each cost is for a single unit. Total costs are computed by extending material, labor and overhead by the quantity produced for each product. The profit margin is a percentage that, when multiplied by the total cost, gives the dollar profit. Find and print the ten products with the highest dollar profit.

   PROD contains:

Product Number	nnnnn
Material Cost	nnn.nn
Labor Cost	nnnn.nn
Overhead Cost	nnnn.nn
Quantity	nnnn
Profit Margin	.nn

2. An automobile manufacturer maintains a file of records showing the number of vehicles presently in the shipping yard. This information is recorded by make and model as follows:

Make	xxx
Model	xx
Number of vehicles in shipping	xxxxx

   Transactions come from data records and contain the following information:

Make		xxx
Model		xx
Code	1 - Delete master record	x
	2 - Add new master record	
	3 - Vehicle going into shipping	
	4 - Vehicle leaving shipping.	

   Write a program to update the existing master file with the transaction records. This process should create a new master file output and a report that shows the latest status of the vehicle records.

3. A bank maintains a sequential file for all of its customers with a savings account. This file contains the following data:

Account Number	xxxxxxx
Date of Last Update	xxxxxx
Present Balance	xxxxx.xx
Balace at Last Month's End	xxxxx.xx
Customer Name	15 characters
Customer address	30 characters

Updating transactions are read from data records in the following format:

Account Number	xxxxxxx
Date of transaction	xxxxxx
Amount	xxxxx.xx
Code 1 - New Account	x
Code 2 - Deposit	
3 - Withdrawl	
4 - Closing Account.	

In the case of a new account, a name and address must be provided by the transaction. These follow the code in the data record.

Write an update program to create a new master file employing the following considerations:

a) There may be any number of transactions per master record with any number of codes.

b) Data records are coded within account number sequence.

c) An overdraft is an error, and a message must be printed if one occurs.

d) There will not necessarily be updating for each master record.

e) A new account may be followed by other transactions.

f) On any given program run, END OF FILE may occur first on either the transaction file or the master file. Make provision for both possibilities.

Appendix A
Computer
Terminals

There are two types of computer systems that most users of BASIC will encounter:

1.   Minicomputers or maxicomputers, which may have a choice of programming languages and whose facilities may be shared by many other users.

2.   Personal computers or microcomputers, which use only BASIC language and have only one user at any one time.

On a system where several users may be connected at once, each user usually has an identification code and must give a "password" in order to gain access to the computing facility. An example of such a procedure appears in Appendix C.

On a microcomputer, the user is not required to pass the "identity test" in order to use the system. As soon as the computer has been turned on, a program may be written and/or executed.

Two types of devices are commonly used to handle the exchange of information and commands between the computer and the user. Both of these have a keyboard, like that of a typewriter, that is used to type commands and data for the computer. The devices differ in that the video display, or CRT (cathode-ray tube) displays the output from the computer on a screen similar to that of a television, whereas the teletype prints the output on paper, like a typewriter. Figure A.1 shows a typical CRT, and Figure A.2 shows a terminal with a keyboard printer.

On both terminals, the keys are positioned much like those of a typewriter, but with the addition of several control functions that are not required on a typewriter. The following chart shows the use of several of the important control keys. On any specific keyboard, the control keys may differ in position and function. Consult the documentation of your particular keyboard for its specifications.

Key	Function
RETURN	Causes a carriage return and a line feed; also transmits the command or statement on that line to the computer.
	The backspace key. Used to correct typing errors before pressing RETURN. For every arrow, one character is deleted.
BREAK	Interrupts the current and returns the system to READY status. The user may now enter a command.
LINE FEED	Advances the paper one line.
CTRL	Used in conjunction with some characters on the keyboard for specific control functions. For example,

CTRL and X are used on some terminals to delete the entire line that has just been typed. The particular characters vary from one terminal to another.

FIGURE A.1 Display Screen and Keyboard *(Courtesy of Cincinnati Milacron)*

FIGURE A.2   Keyboard Printer Terminal *(Courtesy General Electric)*

Appendix B
System
Commands

As in other aspects of computer usage, different systems may have specific commands that are unique, but many commands are almost universal. The following chart shows, in alphabetical order, some of the common system commands and their meanings.

Command	Meaning
BYE	The user is signing off.
CATALOG	Print a list of all programs that have been stored on the computer system by this user. These programs are stored in a "place" sometimes called a library.
LIST	Print all the statements of the program that is currently being used or written. LISTNH on some systems means *No Heading*.
LOAD program name	On some personal computers, this command causes a search, possibly on a cassette tape, for a particular program. The program, when found, is read into main storage and can be listed or executed.
LOGIN or LOGON	On some larger computers, the user initiates communication by one of these commands.
NEW program name	Indicates that a new program is to be written. Main Storage is cleared so that the new program will not be merged or confused with the previous program.
OLD program name	The program name in the command is to be retrieved from the user's library.
RUN	Execute the program that is currently in main storage. If there are no errors, execution occurs. RUNNH means *No Heading* on some systems.
SAVE	Store the current program in the user's library.
SCRATCH or CLEAR UNSAVE	Erase the current program from main storage. program name,
DELETE, PURGE or KILL	Delete the program named from the user's library.

Appendix C
A
Typical
Sign
on
Procedure

When a user signs on to a host computer, there is usually a "greeting" of some kind from the computer system that indicates that the terminal has been turned on. This recognition often includes a company or school name and usually the time and date. After this, beginning, different systems have particular procedures, but the following is typical.

Typed by the Computer	*Typed by the User*
1. Recognition — sign on time and date	
	LOGIN (or LOGON) (not required on some systems)
2. USER ID	
	The user's identification number or code, then RETURN key
3. PASSWORD	
	A code, which must be known in order to gain access to the computer, then RETURN key
4. SYSTEM (not printed by some systems)	
	BASIC, then RETURN key
5. NEW OR OLD (not printed by some systems)	
	Type NEW if a new program is to be written or OLD if a program is to be retrieved from the library, then RETURN.
6. FILE NAME (not printed by some systems)	
	The name of the program, then RETURN. (If NEW were typed above, the computer is now prepared to receive it. If OLD were typed, the library would be searched, and the program with the name given here would be retrieved.)
7. READY	
	If a program is to be written, enter each statement, pressing RETURN after each.

221

Appendix D
Entering
a
Program

When BASIC system is used, new programs may be entered and saved for future use, or old programs may be used in order to obtain certain results from the computer. The following sequence is intended to show both of these operations in a "typical session" with a computer. The comments on the right are explanatory and, of course, are not part of the computer—user interaction.

We will begin by indicating that a new program is to be written.

NEW

Indicate that a new program is to be written

NEW FILE NAME:SAMPLE

READY

```
10   PRINT "TYPE IN THE AMOUNT AND THE INTEREST RATE"
20   INPUT A,R
30   LET S=A*R/100
40   PRINT "THE AMOUNT OF INTEREST EARNED IS";S
50   PRINT "WANT ANOTHER? TYPE '1'"
60   INPUT D
70   IF D=1 THEN 100
80   END
RUN
```

Test the program

?ERROR IN STATEMENT 70 NO LINE NUMBER 100 There was an error in line 70.

READY

```
70 IF D=1 THEN 10
RUN
```

Type the correction

```
TYPE IN THE AMOUNT AND THE INTEREST RATE
?10000,8
THE AMOUNT OF INTEREST EARNED IS 80
WANT ANOTHER? TYPE '1'
TYPE IN THE AMOUNT AND THE INTEREST RATE
?1000,8.75
THE AMOUNT OF INTEREST EARNED IS 87.5
WANT ANOTHER? TYPE '1'
```

Program results are as expected.

```
?2
READY
```

SAVE

Store the program in the library.

225

READY

NEW

NEW FILE NAME:NEXT

READY

} Indicate that a new prog is to be written.

At this point, the computer is prepared to accept a new BASIC program. The old program has been erased from the main storage of the machine. This new program is entered in the same way as the first and can be saved for future use if desired.

If the program called SAMPLE were required by the user, it could be recalled and used. Changes could be made at this point if necessary, and the program could then be saved in its new form or left in the library in its old state.

To recall the old program, the following commands are used:

OLD

OLD FILE NAME:SAMPLE

Bring back the program called SAMPLE from the library.

READY

LIST

Print the statements of the program.

```
10   PRINT "TYPE IN THE AMOUNT AND THE INTEREST RATE"
20   INPUT A,R
30   LET S=A*R/100
40   PRINT "THE AMOUNT OF INTEREST EARNED IS";S
50   PRINT "WANT ANOTHER? TYPE '1'"
60   INPUT D
70   IF D=1 THEN 10
80   END
```

READY

RUN

TYPE IN THE AMOUNT AND THE INTEREST RATE

?2500,10

THE AMOUNT OF INTEREST EARNED IS 250

WANT ANOTHER? TYPE '1'

?2

} The results of program execution.

READY

BYE

} Sign off

At the end, it was not necessary to use another SAVE operation since no changes were made to the program. The program is still in the library and remains there until it is deleted.

Appendix E
American
Standard
Code
for
Information
Interchange
ASCII

The ASCII code (Figure E.1) is an 8-bit code that uses zeroes and ones to represent numerics, alphabetics and special characters. The ASCII code is used as the internal representation for characters in many types of microcomputers as well as a means of coding data for transmission to remote computers. Its primary use in BASIC is for the ASC and CHR$ functions.

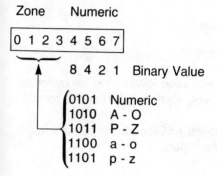

Zone   Numeric

| 0 1 2 3 4 5 6 7 |

8 4 2 1   Binary Value

0101   Numeric
1010   A - O
1011   P - Z
1100   a - o
1101   p - z

FIGURE E.1   ASCII Bit Configuration

Numeric values are recorded in ASCII using the zone 0011 with the corresponding binary value in the numeric portion. The number 7 has the following configuration of ones and zeroes.

0 1 2 3 4 5 6 7   Bit Positions

| 0 1 0 1 0 1 1 1 |

8 4 2 1   Binary Value

7 in ASCII

An alphabetic character uses the appropriate zone, depending on the letter recorded and whether it is upper or lower case. The letter sequence is recorded in binary in the numeric part of the byte. This binary value runs from 1 to 15 in decimal notation, which is equivalent to 0001 to 1111 in binary. Upper case J is recorded as:

0 1 2 3 4 5 6 7   Bit Positions

| 1 0 1 0 1 0 1 0 |

8 4 2 1   Binary Value

J in ASCII

Notice that the numeric portion for J is 1010 or ten in decimal notation since J is the tenth letter in the alphabet. The letter O is the 15th letter and has the code 1010 1111; the 15 is recorded as 1111 in the numeric portion of the byte. Lower case j is recorded as:

0 1 2 3 4 5 6 7   Bit Positions

| 1 1 0 0 1 0 1 0 |

     8 4 2 1   Binary Value

           j in ASCII

In some microcomputers, the lower case letters may be optionally used to represent graphic characters, which may be used to produce charts or to play games.

Figure E.2 shows the complete ASCII code for numeric digits and for upper case alphabetic characters.

Numeric	ASCII	Alphabetic	ASCII
0	0101 0000	A	1010 0001
1	0101 0001	B	1010 0010
2	0101 0010	C	1010 0011
3	0101 0011	D	1010 0100
4	0101 0100	E	1010 0101
5	0101 0101	F	1010 0110
6	0101 0110	G	1010 0111
7	0101 0111	H	1010 1000
8	0101 1000	I	1010 1001
9	0101 1001	J	1010 1010
		K	1010 1011
		L	1010 1100
		M	1010 1101
		N	1010 1110
		O	1010 1111
		P	1011 0000
		Q	1011 0001
		R	1011 0010
		S	1011 0011
		T	1011 0100
		U	1011 0101
		V	1011 0110
		W	1011 0111
		X	1011 1000
		Y	1011 1001
		Z	1011 1010

FIGURE E.2   American Standard Code for Information Interchange

Appendix F
Functions

Functions are powerful commands in BASIC that permit us to perform operations that are either too complex to write ourselves or operations that simply could not be done with the existing commands available in BASIC. For example, we could write a program to find the square root of J, but it is far easier and more efficient to write:

50   LET A = SQR(J)

In this statement, SQR is called the function. The variable J, which supplies the value, is called the argument. Most functions use only one argument, but some string functions use two or three arguments.

ABS(n)

This function supplies the absolute value of the argument n. For example, the statement

40   A = ABS(-15)

supplied the value 15 to A, and:

40   M = 23.5
50   K = ABS(M)

supplied 23.5 to K. However, if M had been -23.5, the positive value 23.5 would also have been established.

ASC(s)

The ASC function returns the equivalent ASCII code for the first character in the string supplied as an argument. For example, the statement:

10   N = ASC("APPLE")

causes the ASCII code for the letter A to be placed in N. Notice that the value in N will be numeric.

ATN(n)

This function finds the arctangent of the value supplied in the argument. The result is in radians. For example, the statement:

70   A1 = ATN(K)

supplies the arctangent of K in radians to A1.

CHR$(n)

This function is the reverse of ASC. In this case, the argument supplies the ASCII code that is converted to the equivalent character. For example, the statement:

100   A = CHR$(L)

takes the ASCII code contained in L and produces the equivalent character in variable A.

COS(n)

The cosine of n is computed and returned by the function. The value n must be expressed in radians.

40   PRINT COS(K)

EXP(n)

The EXP function computes e^n and returns the result.

70   A = EXP(R)

INT(n)

This function returns the integer portion of a fractional number. For example, the statement:

10   R = INT(7.15)

supplies the number 7 to R, having truncated the .15.

LEFT$(s,n)

This two-argument string function returns the n left-most characters from string s. For example, in the statement:

50   IF LEFT$(A$,1) = "Y" GOTO 100

if A$ contains the value YES, then the expression is true since the one left-most character of string A$ is the character Y.

LEN(s)

This function determines the length of a character string, i.e. the number of characters in that string. For example, in the statement:

$$A\$ = \text{``APPLES AND ORANGES''}$$
$$X = LEN(A\$)$$

the value assigned to X is 18.

LOG(n)

This function finds the natural (base e) logarithm of the variable n. The statement:

$$W = LOG(X)$$

computes the natural logarithm of the variable X and assigns the result to W.

MID$(s,n,m)

This is a three-argument string function. It permits the programmer to extract a string from s of length m starting at character n. For example:

```
30   A$ ="10APRIL1980"
40   M$ =MID$(A$,3,5)
```

statement 40 takes 5 characters from A$ starting at position 3 of the string. This action places the name of the month APRIL into M$.

RIGHT$(s,n)

This string function returns the right-most n characters from s. For example:

```
80   A$ ="10APRIL1980"
90   Y$ =RIGHT$(A$,4)
```

these statements place the year 1980 into Y$. Although this could be accomplished with the MID$ function, it is easier to use RIGHT$ since it only requires two arguments.

RND(n)

This function may be used to produce random numbers. Since the characteristics of the random numbers generated may vary from one machine to another, it is suggested that a test program be run using positive, negative and zero arguments. Observe the differences in the results. For example, for a positive argument try:

```
10   FOR I = 1 TO 10
20   PRINT RND(165)
30   NEXT I
```

SIN(n)

The sine of the argument n is returned by this function. The value of n must be expressed in radians.

$$10 \; X = SIN(T)$$

SGN(n)

This function determines the sign of the argument. If the value supplied is positive a 1 is returned. A negative returns −1 and a zero returns zero.

$$40 \; N = SGN(J)$$

When J contains 2.75 a 1 is assigned to N. A −1 is assigned for a value of −37.05 in J.

SQR(n)

This is the function which finds the square root of an argument.

$$55 \; F = SQR(N+D1)$$

This example shows an expression as an argument. First the expression N+D1 is computed. Then the square root of the result is found and placed in F. If N had been 10.5 and D1 was 20.1 then the statement would find the square root of 30.6 and store the answer in F.

Index

f

g

S